TOUGH

CUSTOMERS

Counseling
Unwilling
Clients,
2nd Edition

everly K. Welo, **Editor**

Printed in the United States of America by Graphic Communications, Inc. Upper Marlboro, MD

For information on publications and videos available from ACA, contact our worldwide web home page at: http://www.aca.org

ISBN 1-56991-146-0
This publication may be ordered from:
American Correctional Association
4380 Forbes Boulevard
Lanham, Maryland 20706-4322
1-800-222-5646

Library of Congress Cataloging-in-Publication Data
Tough customers : counseling unwilling clients/edited by Beverly Welo.–2nd ed.
    p. cm.
  Includes bibliographical references and index.
  ISBN 1-56991-146-0 (pbk.)
  1. Resistance (Psychoanalysis) 2. Psychotherapist and patient. I. Welo, Beverly Kay.
RC489.R49 .T68 2001
616.89'14–dc21   2001034339

Dedication

This book is dedicated to my children; Ivar, Nada, and Brian. With love and appreciation for your many gifts, your generosity, and your constant support.

— Beverly Welo, editor

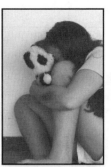

Table of Contents

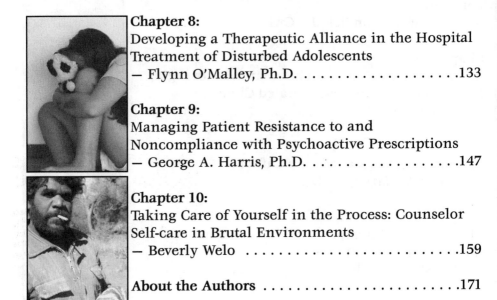

Table of Contents

FOREWORD

By James A. Gondles, Jr., CAE

FOREWORD

Working with adult and juvenile offenders who do not want to be in therapy but have been ordered by the court or some other authority is a difficult task. Therefore, when experts propose strategies to handle this type of client, counselors, caretakers and students should take notice. The original version of this work came out in 1991 and was edited by George A. Harris, Ph.D. We are pleased to issue this second edition of *Tough Customers*, edited by Beverly Welo, the author of another ACA book, *Life Beyond Loss: A Workbook for Incarcerated Men*.

This book will be useful to those professionals who seek new methods of approaching their difficult clients. It explores specific problems faced by counselors and offers a wide variety of approaches from which one can develop his or her own techniques when working with involuntary clients. I recommend reading all the essays even if you are not currently counseling people in a particular group because the techniques noted as viable in one type of setting may be useful in another. The insights and practical techniques offered can be used by counselors in institutions, schools, hospitals, and mental health programs.

Several of the essays are new to this edition and others are updated from the last. They present a variety of ways of assessing clients and interacting with them to achieve the objectives of the counseling sessions. The last essay in the book addresses an often overlooked subject—the needs of counselors who work in restricted settings.

James A. Gondles, Jr., CAE

Executive Director

American Correctional Association

CHAPTER 1

Bringing Them Home to Their Pain:

Beverly Welo
Corrections Program Therapist
TRIAD Chemical Dependency Program
Lino Lakes Correctional Facility
Lino Lakes, Minnesota

Encouraging Introspection in the Incarcerated Client

"We may have civilized bodies and yet barbarous souls. We are blind to the real sights of this world, deaf to its voice; and dead to its death. And not till we know that one grief out-weighs ten thousand joys, will we become what God is trying to make us."

— Herman Melville, *Redburn*

Resistance to introspection is a common problem when working with mandated clients. A variety of factors encourage this resistance. Understanding the global nature of resistance to uncovering painful and difficult memories aids clinicians in creatively responding to their incarcerated clients. Client resistance can then be seen as a fully human response to what C. S. Lewis described as "The Problem of Pain," rather than simple denial of histori-cal fact. This chapter suggests a variety of techniques that may be effectively used to encourage client self-awareness, self-regard, and self-challenge.

Grief and loss counseling provides an opportunity for incarcerated men to look below the surface of their defenses and reconnect themselves with their buried pain. This reconnection can provide an experience of genuine empathy, as it resonates from an understanding of their own emotions. This empathetic response opens an avenue for a fresh connection with other people. It offers a new paradigm for per-ceiving others as fellow suffering grievers. Ultimately, grief work also can help to pro-vide the incarcerated client with a legitimate source of self-esteem. Clients begin to see themselves as empathetic, connected with others, and possessed of the inner strength necessary to deal successfully with highly stressful emotional experiences.

Resistance as a Global Response to Introspection

Before the sequence of events outlined above can occur, client resistance to intro-spection must be resolved. Resistance to looking at buried pain is not a characteristic that is unique to the mandated client. Each of us has avoided emotionally charged memories in many ways. It is necessary for caregivers to be able to acknowledge their own unwillingness, procrastination, and pain avoidance to see client resistance to introspection as a fully human response. By recognizing this resistance as a natural homeostatic reaction to the fear of overwhelming emotional pain, therapists can resist the urge to inappropriately confront client resistance. The desire to confront clients vigorously before a viable therapeutic relationship has developed can then be seen more accurately as a countertransference issue, rather than as evidence of the clients' unamenability to treatment.

All therapeutic journeys are an invitation to experience emotional pain. Traditionally, this "no pain, no gain" analogy has rarely been presented directly to clients—reluctant or seemingly complicit in the process as they may be. In the author's work with involuntary clients in the Minnesota prison system, she has developed techniques to "sell" the reluctant client on this mission. Initially, these techniques may seem more akin to the world of commerce than our traditional understanding of the therapeutic milieu. Nevertheless, they are centered in the historically validated paradoxical intention and distancing components of logotherapy (Frankl, 1962) and make frequent use of the criminal thinking perspective as pioneered by Yochelson and Samenow (1976) and enlarged upon by Walters (1990). The pacing/leading techniques and elements of the victim/perpetrator dialectic as described by Larson and Maddock (1995) also provide important insights for successful development of the therapeutic relationship with the mandated client. She also is indebted to the pioneering work of Salvatore Minuchin (1974) and his "joining" technique, which she has adapted from the family system dynamic to the group context.

Engaging Resistance and Curiosity

The author straightforwardly challenges incarcerated clients during psychoeducational grief and loss lectures by assuring them at the outset that they will experience emotional pain as a result of their decision to take part in grief and loss classes. In addition, she disabuses them of the notion that an understanding of the grief process will result in the somewhat magical "closure" they may have heard described in the pop-psychology terms of their favorite talk show host. This paradox ensures that clients do not strain towards a target idea (such as no longer experiencing uncomfortable emotional responses to the anniversary of a major loss), but rather enjoy the mitigating effects that introspection offers without unrealistic outcome expectations.

For inmates who have only the workbook (*Life Beyond Loss*, Welo, 1999) as a guide, the layout of that material also facilitates a gradual movement to introspection. *Life Beyond Loss* begins with an overview of ten major areas of loss:

- Loss of material goods
- Loss of a job (or role)
- Losses of the physical self
- Loss of control
- Loss of personal freedom
- Loss of relationships
- Loss of childhood

- Loss of spirituality
- Loss through death
- Loss of dreams and goals

These losses are arranged in the order that is likely to be easiest for the client to consider, loss of material goods being less likely to be traumatic than the loss of personal freedom, for example. The text in this chapter is not highly personalized, referring to the more general "incarcerated man's" experience. The first chapter also normalizes the broad range of emotional states that are common to grievers and links the idea of "acting out" as a response to loss. The reader also is introduced to the author's belief that he possesses the ability to choose to end the cycle of acting-out behaviors that led to his incarceration.

The second chapter helps the reader to avoid being overwhelmed by the task of introspection by offering "The Modern View of Death and Loss," a historical perspective on funerary rites, the cultural significance of styles of grieving, the place of gender, and the "Catch 22" of societal expectations of the male response to loss. This chapter also offers the opportunity for the reader to slowly begin the process of introspection by writing a story, imagining he is dealing with a loss at an earlier historical moment. In addition to this encouragement to self-examine, the inmate client is also warned by the text that grief and loss work is a painful and difficult process.

The generalized initial client response to being informed that he will be made uncomfortable is one of distinct confusion. All therapeutic clients hope for a lessening of pain, not an increase in their discomfort. This initial reaction is quickly followed by a stiff-necked resistance to the notion that the therapist could deliver on such a promise. These are men who are used to controlling others with impunity, most frequently through violence or threats of violence. Perpetrators most naturally would cast the author in the role of victim, or possibly that of rescuer (Larson and Maddock, 1995). How is it then, that she is warmly offering them an opportunity to experience their own pain? This forces clients to see the author as Other, thus breaking the interchange free from the victim/perpetrator dialectic and creating a new paradigm for receiving information.

Within this resistance there tends to be a good deal of curiosity. In exit interviews, letters she has received after psychoeducational sessions end, and during casual conversation, inmate clients have told her that they were intrigued because she was clearly "crazy" to tip them off to an expectation of emotional pain. They developed an interest in what her "con" might be, all the while assuming that she could not possibly be seriously offering them pain as an incentive. As one inmate wrote, " . . . when I first started this class I thought it was a bullshit class." The author finds this level of resistance bracing and straightforward, especially in contrast to the compliant client's pseudo interest in the task at hand.

Resistance as "Fear of Fear"

The author invites the client to enter deliberately into this painful situation to paradoxically counteract what Viktor Frankl first described as "fear of fear." Yochelson and Samenow (1976) and Walters (1990) also use this term, in a slightly different context, to describe resistance to introspection in criminal offenders. The assumption in all cases is that resistance is engaged by the belief that the result of facing fear will be overwhelming to the client.

Criminal thinking theory stresses that the criminal client fears he will be reduced to a "zero state" if he experiences emotional pain. The zero state is similar to Gershon Kaufman's (1992) term "shame spiral." Those who work with the individuals Walters describes as "lifestyle criminal offenders" can see the zero state as the nadir of the shame spiral. Other feelings associated with grief (including sadness, confusion, and loneliness) also may prompt this overwhelming sense of hopelessness. By assuring the clients from the outset that their experience will be painful, resistance is paradoxically diminished, in direct proportion to the energy they marshal in an effort to prove the therapist wrong.

Acknowledging Client Vulnerability

Because she works in an environment where her client's emotional vulnerability can legitimately place them at risk, she also provides clients with a variety of therapeutic safety measures. These distancing techniques reassure clients that they will be able to moderate the potentially deleterious effects of their introspection. Safety measures further solidify the therapist in the role of Other, as clients recognize their concerns have been seen as valid and appropriate to the task at hand. Paradoxically, they also elevate the importance of the grief and loss work by spelling out the power implicit in introspection.

By suggesting that clients "suit up" before leaving the group or lecture session, she offers them the metaphor of being "zipped up" (Fossum and Mason, 1986) to explain that they can successfully maintain a façade of indifference while they go about their day in the prison routine. The Fossum and Masson model stresses that some individuals "grow up with unclear boundaries, with their zippers on the outside; they believe that they are indeed regulated by others and the outside world." By reminding clients that they have the strength to stay zipped up as they review loss events that ordinarily would prompt shame reactions, she is encouraging a distancing process that directly benefits them.

Clients have expressed their gratitude to her for this device, explaining that they had feared she would make them cry, rendering them unsafe. No longer experiencing her as a victim, these men had made the assumption that she would attempt to perpetrate harm on them. This illustrates the paucity of role development that is available to these clients, without direct challenge to the victim/perpetrator dialectic.

Inmates who use the workbook, without the aid of a grief group or psychoeducational course work, are supported by the text in their knowledge of the prison environment as a difficult place for introspection. The third chapter, "Normal Life and the Cycle of Grief," acknowledges that some episodes of prison violence can be triggered by guilt and shame over losses. It also proposes the idea that admitting to a loss can lessen stress and urges to act out. The chapter uses a simple story line, concerning an inmate's lost pen, to debunk several myths relating to loss. While challenging the stereotype "big boys don't cry," the text reassures the reader by humorously stating, "I'm not suggesting you burst into tears about losing a pen!" The reassurance is followed by an additional challenge/reassurance, "If you learned to deal with loss by being angry or full of rage, it will be difficult to learn a new course of action. Difficult, but not impossible."

Reducing Client Anxiety through Distancing Techniques and Incentives for Participation

To further safeguard clients who attend grief and loss psychoeducational lectures, the author suggests that they ignore their own losses during early lecture sessions. She encourages them to think of the ways the loss material might relate to "the men at Lino," (the 1,000 individuals who are incarcerated in the medium-custody facility at Lino Lakes, Minnesota) rather than focusing their attention on their own losses. By continuously drawing their attention to "the men at Lino" and how those men "might" experience loss events, individual clients can begin to experience their own introspective moments safely. Assignments often take the form of "a story about someone who has experienced this type of loss," to offer clients an additional distance from their written material. When clients later remark, "Hey! This story is about me!" she is always willing to share in their surprise at this unlikely turn of events.

Being offered a variety of incentives for attending grief class also intrigues inmate clients. For example, many of the men initially are more interested in the certificate that shows they have completed a grief and loss class than the course content. It is common in correctional settings to see men with vast collections of certificates from chemical dependency programs, parenting classes, anger management courses, and work preparedness seminars. These inmates believe, and sometimes rightly so, that case managers and release review boards will see these accomplishments as proof that they have attempted to habilitate themselves.

Because this course work typically requires that written assignments be turned in to the corrections staff, a vigorous black-market flourishes, trafficking in assignments that have passed the courses. To eliminate this, she tells the inmates that they will receive a certificate simply for attending, that they may write assignments or not, and if they choose to write assignments, that they may share them with her or keep them entirely confidential. This paradox ensures that she has yet to receive the same assignment twice, and that she typically receives assignments that are both effortful and revealing.

Because this is such an unusual practice, there are frequently a number of inmates who disagree with this vision, saying that it is not fair. This generally opens a lively discussion of fairness, and the opportunity to discuss the center of control and personal empowerment. She continuously underlines the fact that the class is for them and about them, often commenting that, "It's no skin off my nose," if the assignment is done or not done because they are the ones who will benefit from its completion. This technique helps clients avoid the pitfall of trying to please the therapist, an enterprise that drains energy from introspection as it forces clients to guess at the "right" answers. It also helps the helper to remember that he or she may otherwise unconsciously suggest that the completion of grief and loss assignments (or the completion of a chemical dependency or sex offender treatment assignment) will accurately predict an individual's likelihood of recidivating.

Therapist's Belief in the Efficacy of Introspection

"Selling" the inmate clients on the idea of examining their losses begins in earnest with the fourth lecture session. This corresponds to the fourth chapter in *Life Beyond Loss*, "Pain Avoidance and Substance Abuse." Here the clients are introduced to the value of human suffering: the importance of their own pain as guide, teacher, and source for growth. It is incumbent on the caregiver that he or she believes that "necessary pain" contains a healthy process within it prior to encouraging clients on this journey (Leick and Davidson-Nielsen, 1991). If this is not true for the therapist, the author cannot support his or her decision to offer grief and loss work using the *Life Beyond Loss* materials. Presenting grief and loss work is not appropriate for every professional, and great care must be taken to avoid offering clients a journey that the helper is unwilling to take.

Inmates who use the workbook without staff support find the author's voice one of encouragement, helping them to believe in the efficacy of understanding and assessing long-buried pain. The text explains that friends and family members may have mistakenly guided the reader away from the opportunity to grieve his losses:

> *The people who turned you away from your feelings often wanted to save you from your pain. They may have also wanted to stop your pain so that they would not be uncomfortable with their feelings. Again, you have the right to your feelings, even if they make other people uncomfortable.*

The text is also supportive of the journey through "necessary pain" by the use of quotes from inmates who have participated in grief and loss education at Lino Lakes. Their words are found throughout the workbook, alternately challenging the reader ("My wife and kids have been locked up as long as I have.") and encouraging his efforts ("My pain is the only thing I own free and clear. Now, I know it's worth something.").

Encouraging Introspection as an Aid to Compassion

The "Pain Avoidance and Substance Abuse" chapter outlines four "payoffs" for grief work: the development of healthy compassion, increased strength and health (also described as increased flexibility), a more realistic world view, and an increase in healthy self-esteem.

Throughout the workbook, and in daily contact with inmates, the author makes judicious use of slang, occasional profanity, and prison jargon. This is a technique borrowed from Salvatore Minuchin's "joining" theory in working with the family system. She is not suggesting that a helper go beyond his or her threshold of comfort with highly charged language, rather, that the helper who can say, "Nice pair of skids," when the client exchanges his felony fliers for a new pair of shoes at dress-out has indicated interest, attention to the environment, and humor.

To introduce the subject of compassion during lecture, the author offers a guided imagery exercise. She has found that many of the men she works with are extremely uncomfortable with closing their eyes while in a group with other inmates. Again, she does not confront this resistance by demanding compliance. She prefers to "lead" (Larson and Maddock, 1995) by closing her own eyes first. She also offers the men the option of staring straight ahead and letting their vision "blur." The guided imagery would then begin.

"Take a deep, slow breath in through your nose. Slowly exhale through your mouth. Inhale and hold your breath through the count of four. One, two, three, four. Exhale, two three four. Inhale, two, three, four. Exhale, two, three, four. I want you to bring up a picture of the face of the most caring, loving person you know. This person may be living or dead. She may be sister, mother, stepmother, grandmother, aunt, or friend. He may be brother, father, grandfather, uncle or friend. Look into their eyes, see the kindness there, and see the tenderness they have for you. Examine their face closely. Hold their face in your mind's eye. Imagine that you are bringing them a problem. Look at the ways their face shows they are listening to you. See how they let you know, without any words, that they are interested in your problem. (Pause for several seconds.) Now, let the face fade away. Take a deep slow breath in through your nose, two, three, four. Let the breath out through your mouth, two, three, four. Open your eyes."

What follows is a guided discussion of which person's face they saw. Not all of the clients will be willing to discuss this exercise. The author only calls on men who indicate they are willing to speak. Not surprisingly, the individual most often mentioned is a grandparent, or someone who filled the grandparent's role.

The discussion centers on compassion and how people obtain compassion. The inevitable result is that the men come to the conclusion that compassion originates from an individual enduring pain, and thus becoming able to recognize the manifestations of pain in others. This point is driven home several ways, including discussion of the relative lack of compassion that young children evidence.

The discussion is also guided to encompass the role of bitterness and blame in preventing the development of compassion. Emotional or physical suffering in and of themselves are not described as promoting compassion. Rather, the individual qualities of experience, attitude towards life, faith, and endurance are discussed as central to a compassionate worldview. The use of chemicals to avoid necessary pain is also discussed, as is the link between this form of pain avoidance and the immature (hence uncompassionate) personality.

The men also are asked if the face they summoned up was the face of the sexiest or wealthiest or toughest person that they have ever known. Inevitably, it was not. Yet, without exception, they also are able to identify that the individuals they viewed as the most compassionate were also powerful people, and that strength and perseverance is evident in healthy empathetic people. The discussion is lead to the topic of "attractiveness," which the author defines as the qualities that draw us toward an individual, and specifically the attraction that we all feel towards compassionate individuals. She points to the power of attraction in making friends, getting and keeping a job, and being welcomed into new situations. The discussion also challenges the criminal code of "mistaking kindness for weakness" (Yochelson and Samenow, 1976) by accurately portraying healthy compassionate people as both strong and insightful.

Naturally, attraction is also a key to initiating sexual relationships and the discussion invariably leads to a discussion of sexual attraction as well. This part of the discussion is often timed to end the lecture on a humorous note, with tales of misalliances, which continued despite one or the other partner being someone who would be considered stereotypically "unattractive."

Inmates who are reading *Life Beyond Loss* find compassion described this way:

Working through your pain allows you to experience compassion for the pain of others. Compassion for others is one of the most attractive traits a potential partner has. You may have adopted a self-centered or cynical view of the world out of fear. To break the cycle of unhealthy relationships, showing compassion for others is the first step. To do this you need to use the knowledge that you have gained about your own pain to understand how others may be hurt.

Encouraging Introspection as Integral to Strength and Health

After establishing that a willingness to experience our "necessary pain" results in the specific development of compassion, and that healthy compassion is a universally attractive trait, discussion of a new paradigm of strength and health easily follows. Strength with compassion is described as offering increased flexibility, skill in compromise, increased problem-solving ability, patience, and endurance. All of these adjectives and phrases, as well as additional material culled from discussion, are written on the board. The men are invited to review these traits. When asked if these traits accurately describe themselves, very few inmates have been willing to raise their hands. Those who do are the subjects of laughter from their peers. The men are always ready to assert that they would like to be seen as possessing these qualities, and are frequently able to acknowledge that they have attempted to feign them in the past, to accomplish seduction or other gain.

The discussion is then directed to the criminal thinking trait of "cognitive indolence" (Walters, 1990). The author also uses terms such as "doing life on the cheap" or "flabby thinking," and contrasts this with the Alcoholics Anonymous adage, "doing life on life's terms."

Inmates who use the workbook without staff guidance are offered the following explanation of emotional strength and health:

Many incarcerated men spend a lot of time becoming physically stronger in prison. They show a lot of self-discipline as they try to attain their goals. That strength can attract people to you who like the surface look of who you are. Emotional strength attracts people who see beneath the surface.

The healthier you are, the healthier the people you attract are. Healthy people are more able to build committed relationships. They are more worthy of your trust.

Compassion, health, strength, and flexibility are described as goals obtained by "exercising," and the workbook's assignments are labeled "exercises." The analogy of a workout is used because the gym is traditionally the arena where inmate-clients have shown the greatest endurance, self-discipline, and ability to imagine themselves as experiencing pain for gain. In another nod to Minuchin's joining theory, the author appoints herself as "spotter" in this enterprise. The spotter is defined as a coach who encourages development, as well as one who is implicitly given leave to be directive and confrontive.

Minuchin further defines this role: " . . . the therapist must maintain the authority and mobility of a leader. He will challenge and undermine the patterns that have become stereotyped, limiting the family members' experience." As "spotter" to the inmate client, the author is assuming a similar role, among group members, to Minuchin's role in a family system. She exhorts the clients to do the exercises, but only for themselves. She reminds them about "no pain, no gain," but continuously acknowledge that they can "quit the gym" if they choose to do so.

Encouraging Introspection as a Tenet of Realism

Continuing to discuss the "payoffs" of experiencing necessary pain through introspection leads to the subject of "realism" as a benefit for those who do not continue to avoid the pain of their losses. Realism is also described as "the true gem," or "the real deal." Realistic people are described as "on their square," rather than "looking over their shoulders," or "driving with the rearview mirror"—watching for the police. A realistic worldview also is described as predicated on a substantial fund of self-knowledge, including knowledge of limitations, knowledge of risk factors (such as relapse/reoffense warning signs), and the ability to self-challenge.

Her clients see being realistic as a part of being "a real man." They attempt to portray themselves as fearless realists, but discussion inevitably points out their fear of vulnerability and their unrealistic expectations of self and others. This discussion also touches on the "highly stereotypic sex-role behaviors" that Fossum and Mason see in shame-bound individuals and the Paul Kivel "Man in the Box" model from his *Men's Work* (1992) materials. The discussion proceeds to the statement, "In life there is loss, and with loss there is pain"—unless the pain is avoided through chemical use, violence, or other "unrealistic" coping methods.

She encourages the inmates to tell some of the stories they have heard "other guys" tell about "what they got on the outs" (these are the mythic tales of money, cars, and beautiful women that inmates supposedly have waiting for them when they are released). After a few of these stories, the author suggests that men who actually think they will get to ride in one of these automobiles raise their hands. After the laughter subsides, the discussion is guided to a realistic view of what most ex-inmates will face, and why realistically facing up to what is waiting for them is crucial to combating recidivism. Realism is also described as an attractive trait, and one that is likely to attract a different group of people towards each man. A mock lonely-hearts column letter is then written:

> *I am a compassionate, flexible, realistic*
> *man. I know that pain is a part of life,*
> *that I don't have all the answers and*
> *that it's my job to take care of me.*

When asked who might be likely to respond to such an ad, the most common response is people who are "different" from those who answer more conventional ads. Realism is then further discussed in terms of attraction, both with regards to the qualities the men are attracted to in others and the qualities they currently possess. The price of realism is repeatedly stressed as being the willingness to endure the pain of self-examination.

Inmates who use the workbook without staff guidance are offered the following explanation of the "realistic" world view:

Take a hard, honest look at what you have lost in your life. This will make everything (and everybody) that you have left in your life become more precious to you. People respect the realistic man who does not live in a world of delusion.

By accepting the world in a more realistic way, you no longer try to make potential partners "perfect." No individual can fulfill all your needs. It is unrealistic to search for a partner who will do this. It is unfair for you to demand this from someone else. Again, it is very attractive to potential partners to see you as a realistic person who is able to feel fulfilled in a variety of ways—not just this one exclusive relationship.

Encouraging Introspection as a Method for Building Self-esteem

Self-esteem has been introduced as the last of the "pay-offs" for experiencing our necessary pain through grief and loss work. The author begins this discussion by exposing some of the common myths about self-esteem, such as the belief that healthy self-esteem means "you feel good about yourself all the time." She also speaks about the "props" that often are used to buttress a shaky self-image, such as money, multiple sex partners, drugs, guns, and violence.

Ultimately, she poses a simple theory to her clients: self-esteem comes from doing "the right thing," even when it is the more painful choice. Even within the prison system, very few clients are without the conscience to understand this paradigm. Doing the right thing (rather than the easy, profitable, or malicious thing) is the straightest road to a good night's sleep. Combining it with compassion, flexibility, and realism produces individuals who are comfortable in their place in life, even if their current surroundings are painful.

Inmates who have only the workbook as guide also receive the message that, "Doing the right thing (even when it is painful) is the only way to get stronger." The author's voice remains encouraging, but from the fourth chapter on, it also challenges more directly. An inmate-client who has read that far into the workbook is seen as ready for this deepening of the "therapeutic relationship" with the book itself. The fourth chapter also contains a "good-bye letter" that was written by an inmate to his deceased infant daughter. The letter is an affecting, powerful document. Inmates frequently comment on the power of the letter and their understanding of the compassion, strength, realism, and self-esteem that the writer displayed. The fourth chapter is seen as the turning point for many men regarding their willingness to continue to do the grief work the book outlines. For those who continue in the process, the last four chapters, "Grief and Incarceration," "Denial and Protest," "Grief Proper and Acceptance," and "Reinvestment and Resolution" are all predicated on the assumption that the inmate-reader has made the decision to self-examine.

Limits of Introspection as a Therapeutic Tool

Encouraging introspection through grief and loss work is not a panacea for the revolving door of recidivism. It is simply one element that potentiates internal change in the incarcerated man. The majority of men who are currently incarcerated in the United States will be returning to our communities. Grief and loss work provides a vehicle for introspection that appears (in conjunction with chemical dependency and sex offender treatment) to offer incarcerated men the opportunity to view themselves as a part of the larger fabric of humanity. The goal of this work is to promote empathy in a population that has shown itself to be decidedly unresponsive to the pain of its victims. If even one individual, who would otherwise be victimized, is spared that fate because an ex-inmate saw his potential victim as a fellow suffering griever, the author's work will have achieved its goal.

REFERENCES

Fossum, M. A. and M. J. Mason. 1986. *Facing Shame/Families in Recovery*. New York: W. W. Norton and Company.

Frankl, V. E. 1960. Paradoxical Intention: A Logotherapeutic Technique. *American Journal of Psychotherapy*. 14:520-35.

_____. 1962. *Man's Search for Meaning: An Introduction to Logotherapy*. Boston: Beacon Press.

_____. 1978. *The Unheard Cry for Meaning: Psychotherapy and Humanism*. New York: Simon and Shuster.

Kaufman, G. 1992. *Shame/The Power of Caring, 3rd Edition*. Rochester, Vermont: Schenkman.

Kivel, P. 1992. *Men's Work*. Center City, Minnesota: Hazelden.

Larson, N. R. and J. W. Maddock. 1995. *Incestuous Families*. New York: W. W. Norton and Company.

Leick, N. and M. Davidsen-Nielsen. 1991. *Healing Pain: Attachment, Loss and Grief Therapy*. London: Routledge.

Lewis, C. S. 1962. *The Problem of Pain*. New York: Macmillan.

Minuchin, S. 1974. *Families and Family Therapy*. Cambridge, Massachusetts: Harvard University Press.

Walters, G. 1990. *The Criminal Lifestyle: Patterns of Serious Criminal Conduct*. Newbury Park, California: Sage Publications.

Welo, B. K. 1999. *Life Beyond Loss: A Workbook for Incarcerated Men, Revised Edition*. Lanham, Maryland: American Correctional Association.

_____. *Raging Grievers: A Caregiver's Guide to Providing Grief and Loss Work for Incarcerated Men*. Unpublished manuscript.

Yochelson, S. and S. Samenow. 1976. *The Criminal Personality: A Profile for Change*. New York: Aronson.

CHAPTER

2

George A. Harris, Ph.D.

Psychologist in Private Practice

PsychLogic

Kansas City, Missouri

Overcoming Resistance

with Difficult Clients

Resistance to the therapeutic relationship is a given with many of the most difficult mandated clients. Whatever forms this resistance takes (from the outright aggressive client to the seemingly compliant or passive client), helpers need a diversity of approaches. Each response must be tailored both to the clinician's therapeutic style, and to the special needs of each workplace. This chapter explores many such approaches and challenges and encourages readers to see the role that the therapist's personal expectations of treatment outcome may play in the client's ability to change.

Counselors can learn techniques to overcome problems posed by difficult clients. Readers should recognize that using an eclectic grab bag of techniques may result in a hodgepodge approach to therapy with little focus or direction. So, it is wise to proceed with caution. However, most therapists probably have at least some conceptualization of their cases and can select techniques that are consistent with that conceptualization. With that in mind, let us begin by discussing some principles for working with difficult clients. Discussion of techniques can proceed within the context of these basic principles.

Set Expectations and Provide Structure

Two general principles of good therapy are to set expectations and to provide structure. Clients intent on subverting counseling can do so regardless of how explicit the counselor has been about such matters as appointment time, conduct in sessions, fees, objectives of sessions, and so on; thus, it is hopeless to try to clarify all the ground rules, especially in the initial session (Strean, 1985).

Nevertheless, some rule setting may provide a basis for making clear decisions (Goodyear and Bradley, 1980). Contracts between counselor and client are useful, but only when the client has truly participated in writing the agreement. Enright and Estep (1973) structured counseling by requiring clients who were ordered to complete a set number of sessions to meter their time. When not working productively, the meter was not allowed to run, thus extending the client's stay in therapy.

Other authors (Beck, et al., 1993) recommend that every session should have a set agenda and that the therapist should provide a bridge between the present and the last session. Such structure may be too rigid for some therapists, but with managed care and limits on the number of therapy sessions, it is probably wise not to let therapy wander too much. On the other hand, many therapists find that a loose structure allows clients to gravitate toward issues that they really need to discuss and that too tight a structure is inhibiting. The counselor should consider this issue and make a decision on it based on the client and the counselor's style.

Maximize Choice, Minimize Demand

The principle of maximizing choice and minimizing demand also is helpful in working with treatment-resistant clients. When clients are reactive to coercion, they resent having their choices limited. Therefore, it may be helpful to try to give clients as many choices as possible about appointment times, topics to cover in sessions, and fee arrangements. Whenever possible, it is useful for the counselor to communicate the idea that the client has choices (although a choice between two negative options will hardly seem to be a choice to the client).

Seldom is it a good idea in the first session to spell out for the client all the changes that need to be made. Such laundry lists are discouraging to most treatment-resistant clients. They only see the mountains of work ahead and not the benefits. Solution-oriented approaches often avoid this problem by looking forward rather than backward. Homework assignments should be simple and manageable. When homework assignments are reviewed, counselors should take care not to chastise clients for failure to work, though it is often helpful to explore the resistance behind clients not completing assignments.

Allow Clients to Save Face

Another general principle for working with treatment-resistant clients is to help them save face whenever possible. Nobody likes to be brow-beaten. Selekman (1993) discussed how drug-using adolescents are very resistant to being labeled addicts or alcoholics, and this is true for most adults as well. Avoiding pejorative labels is helpful in discussing the process of counseling. Instead of referring to the sessions as psychotherapy, it may be beneficial to call the work counseling or discussions. The less threatening the label the better. Cognitive therapists might want to refer to clients' irrational beliefs as "controversial,"or "unhelpful," rather than "dysfunctional."

Stimulate Clients to Think

Stimulating clients to think is a broad directive. To accomplish this, therapists may employ techniques that come from many approaches, including family therapy and cognitive behavioral theory. Cognitive therapy generally emphasizes collaboration between client and counselor to approach problems rationally and empirically. Thus, any strategy that helps clients think about themselves and their problem is useful. For example, cognitive therapists (Beck et al., 1993) discussed the uses of Socratic questioning (guided discovery) to help the client shift from externalizing blame to internalizing responsibility. Korn and McKorkle (1959) referred to this technique as detached questioning, the essence of which is to gently ask the client about his role in his predicament and his capacity to independently change what led to the problems.

Cognitive therapists frequently stimulate thinking by use of the advantages/disadvantages technique, which asks the client to list the pluses and minuses of a course of action. Cognitive therapists frequently challenge clients to discuss the evidence for or against a belief. These techniques are useful in creating reflection rather than reaction.

Many techniques from family and strategic therapies also stimulate clients to think. For example, scaling techniques ask clients to rate experiences on a continuum of 1 to 10 or 1 to 100. An adolescent might be asked, for instance, to rate how irritating his parents are on a ten-point scale. By doing so, the therapist interrupts either-or thinking and forces the client into some consideration of complexity. Questions asking clients to identify sequences of events help them to explore and challenge assumptions about linkages.

Circular questions about relationships force thoughtfulness about those relationships. For example, a reluctant probationer might be asked questions such as, "Who would be most likely to be upset if you terminated therapy and violated the terms of your probation?" or "Who would you be least likely to disappoint in your family by not completing your program?" This kind of exploratory questioning can be helpful in stimulating thinking.

Ignore Resistance

Many things are said or done in counseling that would have been better left untouched. For example, if a client in an institutional setting inappropriately attempts to form a special alliance with a counselor by gossiping about another staff member, the best tactic initially may be to change the subject rather than deal directly with the gossip, as long as the remark is mild and unlikely to cause any material consequences. Ignoring the client in this instance may allow time to establish a better relationship that would withstand the tension of a more direct discussion of the inappropriateness of a similar remark later.

Timing is critical. It also may be appropriate to suggest that the client talk directly with the staff member. If the counselor offers to set up a three-way meeting to explore the complaint, most clients will quickly decline and stop complaining.

The counselor also may choose to ignore angry or blaming remarks from clients. Counselors will have different beliefs and approaches to this. Some will prefer to deal with such problems as they arise. Particularly at the beginning of counseling, direct discussion of how the client is externalizing blame may result in the client feeling blamed. Some clients may test their counselors by telling fabricated, exaggerated stories to get shock reactions and to determine whether the counselor will maintain confidentiality. If the story becomes known to other staff members, the client knows who related it.

Regardless of the client's reason, even if it is to see whether the counselor is judgmental or trustworthy, counselors should take everything lightly and withhold reactions until they know more. This is a prudent strategy for avoiding premature termination of counseling because it allows clients to test the waters to see whether they want to come in. Counselors who work as part of a therapeutic team have the ethical obligation to let clients know with whom their case will be regularly discussed.

Create Optimum Anxiety to Stimulate Self-examination

Counselors are trained to work with people who become aware of a problem or get an uncomfortable feeling and ask for therapeutic help. These clients recognize the need for change because they want to feel better or because they realize their situation or problem, if left unchanged, will bring about undesirable consequences. Although they sense something is amiss, they may blame someone else for their unhappiness, anger, or anxiety, or they may view their unwanted situation as caused by factors outside their control. Nevertheless, they seek counseling because they hope to find a way to resolve the issue or because their anger seems unproductive and draining.

The involuntary client, on the other hand, often does not have anxiety or lacks awareness of it. Anger may exist, but the clients do not see this as inappropriate because they believe others are at fault. Most important, the righteousness of the anger prevents the client from considering how self-defeating his anger is. Thus, there is no motivation to change. If clients who are referred involuntarily to counseling do not express their feelings or avidly enlist the counselor to help them change a bad situation, how then should the counselor proceed? One possibility is to try to create anxiety or self-doubt in the person. A way of doing this is to point out inconsistencies between behavior and professed beliefs, or to point out how the person's choice of actions resulted in his present situation.

Another method is to provide feedback about how others view and evaluate the person. The stronger the relationship between the counselor and the client, the more likely such methods will be tolerated by and beneficial to the client.

However, many clients will reject these attempts as unwelcome criticisms. This will be so, particularly, for people who do not develop trust easily. Clients who do not have or are unaware of the usual anxiety also will deflect these techniques. A particular danger in confronting clients before a relationship is formed is that the counselor then becomes the adversary. Clients who are treatment resistant do not give counseling the benefit of a few warm-up sessions, which makes it difficult to time the confrontations appropriately. There is no opportunity for a client/counselor bond to form because the client does not let that happen. The trick is to create the anxiety without being blamed by the client for doing so. Much of the success that comes from doing this depends on style. Some counselors can smile while confronting their clients and the client does not link the negative confrontation with the "friendly" counselor. Nothing sticks to the "Teflon" counselor.

While creating anxiety is often necessary, it is also true that much resistance stems from too much anxiety. Reducing anxiety, then, helps clients relax and take a more measured view of their situation (Young, 1992). One technique for reducing anxiety is to "normalize" the problem. That is, the counselor should point out how many people are in a similar situation and how it is not a great personal aberration. For example, a man may be forced into treatment by his wife, who is upset at the provocative behavior between the father and daughter. The counselor may carefully point out that many men find themselves interested in their daughter's sexual development, but there is a line between appropriate and inappropriate interest that is sometimes crossed. By saying this, the counselor empathizes with the man's criticized feelings while clearly stating that acting on those feelings in sexual ways is inappropriate. The father may be relieved because he may have felt freakish and embarrassed at having feelings he could not prevent. This reduction of anxiety then frees him to explore acceptable ways of channeling his feelings.

Still another way of reducing anxiety is to ask questions in early sessions that do not tap material that is too sensitive. Sometimes taking a family history can be informative as it places the client in his or her social context. Asking a client to describe the personalities of different family members and the client's relationship with them can be revealing, and it is something most people can do without much prompting.

A technique related to creating anxiety is inducing frustration. Erickson (1980) described this technique as prompting a low-intensity response, then inhibiting it before it could be expressed. For example, in a family meeting, a reticent child might be asked a question then denied the opportunity to answer by a quick change of subject. The frustration in the child builds until he is bursting with something to say.

Gestalt therapists create a similar effect by trying to create awareness in the client without giving any indication of how that awareness should be channeled. A counselor might point out how the client is clenching his teeth, but the counselor does not then interpret what the clenching means. The induced awareness of the behavior brings into consciousness the client's unfinished business, which is frustrating, and the client then becomes motivated to resolve what is incomplete. The counselor, who refuses to take responsibility for what the behavior means, forces the client to do so. Thus, Erickson creates tension by inducing awareness of unfinished business (Young, 1992).

Time Interventions for Critical Moments

Another tactic is not to try to create anxiety or discomfort, but to wait until clients are suffering as a natural consequence of their actions, such as catching alcoholics when their world is crumbling around them or criminals when the awesome reality of imprisonment seems imminent. Timing interventions this way tends to keep the counselor out of the adversary role. Unfortunately, however, many counselors want to ease their clients' pain at these moments by offering reassurance or by enhancing their self-esteem. Instead, what is often necessary is a persistent, but not cruel, inventory of the person and assessment of the situation (Samenow, 1984).

Counselors have to learn to do concentrated work while the client is open to it. Weekly sessions may fail because the client's defenses will be reconstructed between sessions. Counselors should not be too harsh on their clients while they are depressed or unhappy, but they should not do their clients' work for them, either. The difficulty with this approach is that it is not preventive, and the client's life is already chaotic before openness to counseling occurs. By then, the crisis tends to turn counseling either into emotional exchanges or to strategizing about how to escape the immediate crisis, rather than attempting to mutually determine the roots of the problem and encouraging the client to accept personal responsibility for it.

Pique Curiosity

A different method of engaging reluctant clients is to intrigue them and pique their curiosity. Yochelson and Samenow (1976, 1977) described how they give clients a lengthy description of their hunches about their behavior and thoughts about work, school, friendships, and family. The accuracy of the unflattering portrait disarms criminals who wonder how someone who does not know them knows them so well.

A variation is to make a prediction about the client's behavior. For example, batterers whose wives have left them are usually distraught and seek counseling because their wives demand it before they will consider reconciliation. Counselors can point out that the man's motivation to continue counseling will dissipate as soon as his wife returns.

Some men are quite aware of their intent but are intrigued with the counselor's insight and conduct (assuming that the counselor has declined requests to strategize about how to get the woman to return rather than how to change the violent behavior). Other men may deny to themselves that they lack a sincere interest in counseling except as a device to get their wives back, but the truth will become clear over time, and the accuracy of the earlier assessment can be pointed out later to weaken the man's self-assured certainty.

Sometimes psychological tests make clients curious and willing to talk, if for no other reason than to satisfy a curiosity about themselves, much like the desire to see pictures of oneself in various poses or costumes. Some clients, however, treat testing as an opportunity to manipulate or make fun of the counselor, and then, the testing results must be treated with caution.

Identify Positive Intent

People who are involuntarily referred to counseling are usually in conflict with other people, either legally or socially. When such a conflict exists, parties to the conflict tend to view each other's motivations negatively. Parents who are having trouble with a rebellious child frequently say the child is being stubborn or selfish. However, it is possible for the counselor to put the child's behavior in a different light and soften hostility by saying he is showing signs of wanting to be independent, a praise-worthy characteristic of anyone soon to become an adult. Many behaviors that are ordinarily viewed negatively are perhaps done for basically positive and humane reasons. If the underlying motivation can be understood, the counselor is in a better position to be empathic and nonjudgmental toward the client, aiding the counseling process.

Identifying positive intent in the involuntary client is a precondition for use of many powerful paradoxical techniques. Tennen et al. (1981) described defiance-based paradoxical prescriptions as successful because the client rebels against the counselor's interpretation of a positively motivated negative behavior. For example, a client who does not say much in therapy might be praised and encouraged to continue to be very thoughtful about what he says. A client who is argumentative in a family meeting might be praised for being so involved and active. Anderson and Stewart (1983), Teismann (1980), and Watzlawick et al. (1967) also offer extended discussions of relabeling, reframing, and positive intent.

Often, the counselor has no actual power to stop a client's behavior. However, if the counselor defines the behavior as positive and insists that it is what he or she wants, the client may stop it. For example, the counselor may be annoyed that during a group counseling session, two group members talk to each other and exclude the other members. The two may be gently teased and encouraged to provide barely audible background noise so that the rest of the group can continue. The counselor then provides feedback on their noise level and lets them know if they are too soft or too loud. By taking control this way, the counselor has prevented the clients from excluding and disrupting the other group members. The counselor may not be able to directly control a behavior but can indirectly do so by changing some part of it.

As implied earlier, perhaps the most important benefit from looking for positive intent in an otherwise negative behavior comes from the increased empathy the counselor can feel toward the client. Clients who appear rebellious, uncooperative, angry, and uncommunicative can be viewed positively as wanting self-determination (Riordan et al., 1978). Counselors who recognize this motivation are less likely to be critical or to try to impose unnecessary restrictions on the client that would increase rebellious behavior and undermine the development of a therapeutic alliance.

Empathy and acceptance of the client are, in fact, the ultimate paradox of counseling. When the counselor understands and acknowledges the reluctance that clients have about changing, clients feel free to change. For example, when the counselor understands that the alcoholic has not quit drinking because of the risk of losing drinking buddies, the client becomes freer to consider quitting as an option. The more the counselor emphasizes the reason for changing, the more the client reacts with the reasons why change is not possible. The more the counselor emphasizes the risks of changing, the greater the client's freedom is to consider the advantages of changing.

While it is important to try to look for the positive intent behind negative behaviors, counselors also need to consider that such intent may not always be present. Yochelson and Samenow (1976, 1977), for example, viewed the motivations of the offender as egocentric and irresponsible. They described the criminal as being interested in the excitement of criminal activity rather than in the dull pleasure of a responsible life. They stated that criminals view themselves as unique people who should not be subjected to the rules that govern ordinary people. The criminal was further described as one who wants power over others for personal benefit.

Juveniles who are truant from school may be unconsciously reacting to stress by trying to attract their parents' attention to keep them from arguing between themselves; children suffer less stress from being truant than from worrying about their parents' arguments. On the other hand, some criminal children may be truant because they are simply bored with the demands of school and prefer the excitement of street life. To be successful at finding positive intent, counselors need to have an understanding of their clients' underlying personality structures and interpersonal interactions. This boils down to understanding what end is served by apparently illogical, self-damaging behavior.

Naive paradoxical prescriptions also should be avoided. For example, suicidal patients should not be instructed to "go ahead and do it." These simplistic prescriptions are not paradoxical at all; they are dangerous.

Use Nonverbal Techniques

Perhaps the most simple thing to try when dealing with a client who is reluctant to talk is to "talk about not talking" by exploring the reasons for staying silent. Sometimes clients have difficulty using language to describe their experiences. One method to use when working with difficult nonverbal clients is to engage them in physical activities, such as crafts, sports, or survival-skill expeditions.

People of all ages and types can learn much about themselves through involvement in survival tests. Situations that expose clients to new stimuli also may have educational value. These are especially useful because clients get caught up in the experience and find themselves participating to survive, emotionally and physically.

Encounter groups using the "hot seat" have a similar quality. Rooney (1992) described work with involuntary clients in groups and families, noting the power of peers to be both positive and negative role models. Much of this social learning is nonverbal and difficult to replicate in individual therapy where the therapist is not necessarily a role model for the client. Learning in groups often is achieved because peers can accept confrontation better from each other than from an authority figure such as a therapist.

Unfortunately, counselors often assume that the client is resistant rather than consider the possibility that they have used an inadequate approach (Lazarus and Fay, 1983). It is too simplistic to always attribute lack of progress in counseling to the client's resistance. Involuntary clients are not as likely as voluntary clients to adapt to the counselor's style. That is, an involuntary client who agrees to participate after some preliminary talking may not remain convinced that counseling is valuable if the counselor's approach does not seem sensible as the sessions progress.

Imagine that a wife talks her husband into trying counseling. The man has a high school diploma and operates heavy machinery for a living. The counselor begins by taking an extensive family history, including information about the couple's parents and grandparents. The wife enjoys this discussion, but the husband does not because he does not see how it relates to their problems. Regardless of how theoretically relevant the information is, a present-focused, action-oriented man who was reluctant to enter counseling in the first place will soon renew his reluctance and resist coming to counseling. It is important, then, to try to adapt to clients rather than stick religiously to an approach that might drive them away.

Capitalize on Various Styles of Learning and Change

People learn in different ways. It is especially important to consider the learning style of the involuntary client. A brief listing of ways that people change should highlight some approaches that counselors may consider.

1. **Insight.** Gaining insight into your own thoughts and behavior is the basis for much counseling, but many people do not change behavior through better cognitive understanding, or they find that understanding hard to achieve. Other methods may be necessary to communicate a message.
2. **Modeling.** Some clients will learn best by seeing the appropriate behavior displayed. Counselors can demonstrate the behavior themselves or arrange a demonstration.

3. **Behavior rehearsal.** This is the "try it, you'll like it" technique. Clients may grudgingly agree to try on a new behavior, then discover they like it. Role-playing often follows demonstration of the behavior and is followed by a real trial of the behavior. For example, a client who needs to learn how to express feeling may observe a counselor's self-disclosure, then practice self-disclosure in role-playing with the counselor before trying to talk openly with friends or family members.

4. **Self-esteem.** Some people improve in all areas of functioning when they feel better about themselves. This enhancement of self-image is most often made possible by achievement and recognition, not direct discussion of self-worth.

5. **Relationships.** Some people improve in the presence of an empathic counselor or friend who allows them to open up and be themselves without criticism or judgment.

6. **Group pressure.** The power of the emotional field of the group and family is strong. Peer cultures may work better than individual therapy. Sometimes it is easier to help the client change by influencing the family first. Sometimes the client may not be able to respond to direct suggestions whereas family members can. Thus, the path of least resistance (and effort) may be through a slightly circuitous route.

7. **Reinforcement.** Much behavior is influenced by reaction to it in the environment. An unresponsive environment inadequately rewards behavior change. It is often difficult for counselors to affect the external environment, but sometimes this is possible. For example, a child having difficulty in school may be helped by having the teacher or principal arrange immediate feedback and praise for slight improvements in the child's behavior that previously may have been overlooked.

The First Session with a Treatment-resistant Client

This section reviews the nuts and bolts for what to do in preliminary sessions. It is broken down into the five following steps:

1. Assess the client.
2. Deal with the issue of involuntariness.
3. Challenge false beliefs.
4. Find a problem on which the client will agree to work.
5. Develop a treatment plan.

Assess the Client

Some type of formal or informal assessment happens in every counseling encounter. Counselor and client size each other up and behave according to their perceptions. It may not be essential to conduct extensive psychological testing. Brief therapy models almost preclude allowing time for such assessment, and problem-and-solution-focused models do not emphasize the importance of personality constructs or the conduct of therapy. However, at a minimum, there should be some assessment of clients' capacity to engage in counseling and their willingness to work.

Clients with formal thought disorders (such as schizophrenia) usually are not good subjects for therapy until they receive psychiatric care, usually medication. The primary recommendation of Meloy et al. (1990) is for counselors of psychiatrically disabled clients to work as part of an interdisciplinary team that includes a psychiatrist.

With this group, much of the counselor's job is to explain to the client the importance of the medication and to work through the client's resistance to taking and staying on medication. As previously noted, the client's resistance to medication may stem from his fears of dependency. Once thought disorders are treated, personality disorders may become more evident. It is important to be prepared for these dual-diagnosis clients.

Many other dual-diagnosis problems exist with resistant clients, and psychiatric help may be useful. Many substance-abusing clients have underlying mood disorders, such as depression, that may be medically treatable. The substance abuse may be an attempt by the client to self-medicate, and it does not make sense to treat the underlying medical problem with psychotherapy. Other conditions are not so clearly biological in origin, but they may still respond to medication. For example, some clients who have anger- or impulse-control problems may respond to mood levelers, and when treated, they often become more amenable to psychotherapy.

Whenever there is any question about whether medical intervention may be helpful, get a medical consultation. It is increasingly apparent that there are biological, psychological, and social influences on behavior, and difficult cases call for a consideration of all possibilities (Lazarus, 1992).

A second important assessment consideration is the extent to which the client has a diagnosable personality disorder. Whether the therapist finds such personality disorder labels useful, these concepts are not meaningless. Clearly, some personalities with a pathological outlook are quite different from most clients. The antisocial client who disregards the rights of others is a case in point. Such clients do not establish true interpersonal bonds. It is usually a mistake to assume that empathy with them will allow the counselor to forge a therapeutic relationship.

Of course, it is important to be clear about appropriate boundaries with all clients. Clients with personality disorders often try to use the counselor's caring as a weapon. For example, the client may try to extract favors and privileges that the counselor should not grant. In a correctional institution, for example, the client may ask to use the counselor's phone. A probationer may ask the counselor to verify attendance at sessions that he did not, in fact, attend. Consequently, from the beginning, the counselor should have some idea whether a client is antisocial in order to be able to select a suitable approach. It is important to be especially clear about appropriate boundaries with these clients.

Though there is much disagreement about this issue, Yochelson and Samenow (1976) are correct in their assertion that the counselor of antisocial clients with criminal personalities must be more dispassionate than empathic. The problems of the personality-disordered client are fairly deeply ingrained. This makes it vitally important that the therapist working with the client in limited sessions clearly specifies issues to be addressed. Otherwise, therapy time becomes scattered and poorly focused as scores of issues bubble up and are minimally addressed in the allotted time.

Effective therapy with personality-disordered clients requires deeper psychotherapy than brief therapy allows. Yochelson and Samenow's (1976) approach required one year of daily three-hour group treatment. If there is not enough time allocated to do this intensive therapy, then therapy goals need to be modified to fit within the allowed schedule.

Therapy goals should be modified to be consistent with the counselor's skill level. In-depth therapy in psychodynamic models involves confronting the client's behavior toward the counselor as a way to examine underlying personality dynamics. Examining this transference is slow and difficult work that many counselors are not prepared to do and do not have time to do.

Other clients have problems in living. These are the clients most counselors see. This broad category includes people with substance abuse problems, though these problems can be as intractable as those of either thought or personality-disordered clients. Dowd and Wallbrown (1993) describe the personality of the psychologically reactant client, including dynamics of motivation and relationships, which are of interest to counselors and therapists. They administered the Therapeutic Reactance

Scale, the Questionnaire for Measuring Psychological Reactance, and the Personality Research Form to 251 undergraduate students. They concluded that the psychologically reactant person tends to be aggressive, dominant, defensive, autonomous, and is quick to take offense. Such persons do not affiliate with others, and do not seek or give support. The reactant person values freedom from restraint.

Though these descriptions sound quite negative, the authors also noted that, in some circumstances, such people might be forceful and effective leaders. They may have great confidence in themselves. They would try to control events rather than be controlled. Counseling would be difficult, because they would not be easily influenced by the counselor.

In the DSM-IV (1994), the diagnosis of passive-aggressive personality disorder was removed. However, this diagnosis in the DSM-IIIR was very descriptive of a large number of reactive, treatment-resistant clients. The DSM-IIIR described these clients as having a pervasive pattern of passive resistance to demands for social and occupational performance. This included procrastinating, becoming sulky and argumentative when asked to do something, working slowly to avoid unpleasant tasks, protesting that demands were unreasonable, "forgetting" obligations, evaluating personal performance higher than others did, resisting suggestions from others, obstructing the efforts of others by failing to participate, and unreasonably criticizing or scorning people in positions of authority.

Given these descriptions of reactant people, it is easy to speculate what problems in living they might have. These might include brushes with authority and difficult interpersonal relationships. Clearly, a major task for the counselor is assessing how reactive a client is and planning an approach in counseling that avoids activating counterproductive behaviors. There is no point in setting unnecessary limits, because this brings about damaging defiance.

Like the antisocial client, the reactant client may have problematic interpersonal relationships. Unlike the antisocial client, the reactant client may have the capacity to form a productive therapeutic alliance. So, it may be helpful to empathize with the reactant client's feelings of anger when he feels constrained or restricted. This is less true with antisocial clients who do not develop any mutuality or sense of reciprocity in relationships.

Deal with the Issue of Involuntariness

A second task in the beginning work with a coerced or treatment-resistant client is to deal with the issue of involuntariness. As previously described, it may be helpful to empathize with the anger the client feels at being coerced into counseling. Empathy tends to further the therapeutic alliance by helping the client to feel understood. Such behavior also helps to disassociate the counselor from the source of the coercion and helps the client understand that the therapist does not mandate the therapy.

The counselor should be careful not to reject the moral or legal basis for the coercion. That is, if the requirement to be in counseling is legitimate, the counselor cannot disagree with the court or authority making the requirement. Nevertheless, it is important to understand the client's feelings. Most counselors do not enjoy wielding power over their clients, though for probation and parole officers and corrections' counselors, power is inherent in the job. However, whenever possible, counselors should disassociate from power and coercion because counseling should empower clients, not control them.

Counselors also should learn whether clients will blame them for the coercion. Counselors should assess how strongly they adhere to their beliefs and should point out that they are not the ones who ordered the counseling to take place. Most clients will recognize this and not be angry at the therapist. Clients who persist in blaming the therapist probably have core issues that will require longer-term therapy and indirect approaches.

When clients acknowledge some responsibility for their predicament, it is possible for counseling to be direct. However, when clients project their problems onto therapists irrationally, the counselor needs to remain somewhat hidden by asking questions, getting information, and encouraging the client to talk. The transference relationship between counselor and client becomes a focus of counseling and also a gauge of progress. That is, the more accurately and realistically the client treats the counselor, the more progress is occurring. Yet, if the client treats the counselor as a parent, difficult problems remain.

Challenge False Beliefs

At some point in counseling, the therapist begins to challenge the client's false beliefs. These challenges may be direct or indirect, depending on the openness of the client to challenge. Reactive clients respond to challenges by locking into a power struggle, but less obvious confrontations may be helpful. Ellis (1985) acknowledged that when vigorous persuasion sets up resistance to the counselor, the counselor should return to relationship building. As long as a client has an external adversary, there is no internal scrutiny. While a head-on clash with the client may be counter-productive, there are other approaches to take to begin to undermine false beliefs.

The false beliefs that undermine participation in counseling fall into three major areas that demand challenging:

- low-frustration tolerance
- discomfort anxiety
- narcissistic resistance

Low-frustration Tolerance. Clients with low-frustration tolerance often believe that they should not have to exert much effort to satisfy the requirements of counseling or to change. Of course, anyone can agree that it would be nice for everything to be easy, but the counselor at least can ask clients why they believe things should be easier than they are. The counselor may need to ask clients if they have such a belief. This method will enable the client to surface the issue and identify it. It is not always necessary to argue that such a belief is untrue, though this direct approach may be effective, at times. Clients who are spending their energy being distressed at how difficult things are seldom have enough energy to apply to actually solving problems, so it is important to deal with their low-frustration tolerance.

Discomfort Anxiety. A second belief counselors need to challenge is discomfort anxiety. Clients with discomfort anxiety often have substance abuse problems and use drugs or alcohol to relieve anxiety caused by a variety of life events. When clients tell themselves, "I can't stand to feel anxious" about a problem or conflict, they solve their problem by treating it with a chemical (Ellis, 1985). Beck et al. (1993) identified a variety of addictive beliefs, such as the expectation that a substance will improve intellectual functioning; increase pleasure; have a soothing effect; relieve boredom, anxiety, tension, and depression; and satisfy cravings. They also identified permission-giving beliefs such as, "Since I'm feeling bad, it's OK to use" and "If I take a hit, I can get away with it," and "I'm entitled." All of these beliefs center around the person's inability to tolerate discomfort.

Since most effective counseling at some time increases discomfort, it is essential to deal with beliefs that impede tolerating discomfort. If the client will permit a direct examination of these thoughts and beliefs without it threatening the therapeutic relationship, then the counselor can ask direct questions and point out the fallacy in the client's thinking. However, if the client is highly reactive and the therapeutic relationship is fragile, then it is more important to challenge the beliefs more subtly by asking what evidence the client has to support the belief. Often, just asking clients to explain themselves is sufficient to provoke an examination that begins to undermine their former thinking.

Narcissistic Resistance. The third category of false belief that counselors must challenge early in counseling is narcissistic resistance to counseling. Clients often believe that they should be able to do what they want, when they want to do it; they should not have to do anything they do not want to do, and they should be treated "fairly." Such clients have difficulties with setting or obeying realistic limits. As long as clients are angry that they are being restricted, it is difficult to get them to examine other changes that they need to make.

Clients who reject limits on themselves seem particularly difficult to engage in counseling because they project blame so readily onto others. Their view is that they would be fine if others would just leave them alone. Sometimes it is helpful to look for exceptions to their rules. That is, ask if there are any circumstances in which conforming to rules is reasonable, such as obeying traffic laws. Most clients will acknowledge the need to obey traffic laws. The counselor, then, can begin to ask what other rules the client finds reasonable and why. These discussions can be philosophical, but they eventually can come full circle to examining the reasonableness of being required to participate in counseling.

Find a Problem on Which the Client Will Agree to Work

It is extremely important to define a problem or goal on which the client agrees to work. When clients voluntarily seek counseling, they come with an issue or feeling they want to change. There may be unconscious roadblocks to change, but at least the client can identify the subject of the counseling. Coerced and treatment-resistant clients see the problems as external to themselves. So, when the counselor asks what needs changing, the client points a finger at someone else who cannot be influenced in the counseling session. The counselor must find a way to frame a topic that can be addressed in counseling.

The art of counseling difficult clients is to gradually shift the responsibility back to the client. One technique for doing this is through detached questioning. In detached questioning, the counselor continues to ask clients to define their role in a problem. For example, if the client denies responsibility for a fight with a friend, the counselor can ask questions to get specific, factual information about the chain of events that led to the fight, including the client's specific behaviors. This can be done without directly implying blame, but the questioning points clearly to the client's involvement.

In the early counseling sessions, the task of finding a mutually agreeable focus is a broad one. It only requires the identification of things that the client wishes were different. The most obvious problem the client has is being under pressure to be in counseling. When clients deny having problems, they usually believe they do not have problems with which they think the counselor can help. The following script demonstrates finding a problem focus:

Counselor: What problems do you want to focus on here in counseling?

Client: I don't know. I don't think I have any problems.

Counselor: Well, it seems to me that one of the problems you have is having to be in counseling.

Client: Well, yeah, but there's nothing you can do about that.

Counselor: Maybe. But I suspect you're angry about it. Do you like feeling angry?

Client: No, but that's the way it is.

Counselor: Do you think it would be worthwhile to see if there's a way to deal with your anger about it constructively?

Client: Maybe.

Counselor: Have you ever been angry before at being made to do something?

Client: Sure, but that's how it is when people force you to do what they want.

Counselor: What different ways have you dealt with that kind of pressure?

Client: Sometimes, I ignore it. Sometimes, I get mad.

Counselor: When you've ignored it in the past, did you get away with it?

Client: Sometimes.

Counselor: So, maybe, what we need to do is figure out when it's safe to ignore demands from other people and when it's not. Do you think everybody hates being forced to do things as much as you do?

Client: Yeah, I guess.

Counselor: How do you know? Is it possible they don't?

Client: Maybe.

Counselor: Maybe it would be helpful to understand why you are particularly sensitive to pressure.

Client: Yeah, I do get pretty mad.

In this scene, the client has been introduced to the notion of using counseling to look at himself and to examine differences between himself and others. Rather than preaching self-responsibility to the client, the counselor tries to frame the problem in a way that allows the client to enter into counseling without losing face. If clients feel boxed in by the questions, their answers will remain terse, so it is important to encourage clients to feel free to express their thoughts and feelings by remaining nonjudgmental.

Many therapists may be making their work with treatment-resistant clients more difficult than it needs to be by ignoring straightforward and simple interventions with these clients. For example, when a client seems to be holding back by not talking, the counselor might try simply reflecting that observation, making the covert become overt. If done nonconfrontationally, the client has the option to deny or acknowledge the observation.

Even if the client denies such behavior, the client knows that the counselor knows what is happening, and the passive-resistant behavior loses some of its power. If clients choose to acknowledge the restraint, the counselor can ask clients why they need to remain silent. Talking about not talking can be a very powerful tool to explore clients' fears about counseling and to identify problems that are the usual focus of therapy. Remember, clients will not identify problems for therapy if they are still resisting the idea of counseling itself.

When clients agree to participate, they only agree to work on issues that they see as important. Many therapists like to develop contracts with clients that spell out the terms of counseling. These contracts are a good idea but only if the client clearly perceives a quid pro quo arrangement; that is, if the contract is forced on the client without the client's input, the contract is useless.

Clients must perceive that they are getting something in exchange for their effort. An example of a flawed arrangement is the typical probation contract that unilaterally spells out the terms of probation. Clients who sign these "agreements" are not really agreeing to anything. They sign because they are forced to, not because they think the arrangement is fair. Consequently, the odds are slim that they will comply with the contract.

Ideally, contracts with clients should be physically written in the client's own handwriting and language. The greater the participation by the client, the greater are the chances for success. In practice, many situations require that the therapist complete the paperwork, but therapists should be aware that the more they do the work, the less the client has invested in the process (Goodyear and Bradley, 1980).

A variation to finding a problem to work on is finding a solution. Selekman (1993) offered suggestions for working with difficult adolescents by employing a brief solution-oriented approach. As with other counseling theories, rapport building is essential, and beginning efforts are aimed at establishing a therapeutic alliance by using self-disclosure, humor, therapeutic compliments, normalizing, and positive relabeling. For example, a withdrawn adolescent can be positively relabeled as thoughtful, or an angry parent's behavior can be portrayed as showing a high level of concern and commitment.

A primary assumption of solution-oriented therapy is that clients have the ability to solve their dilemmas and that problems are unsuccessful attempts to resolve difficulties. Nevertheless, the focus on problems is inevitably negative while focusing on desired outcomes is encouraging and positive. So, instead of dwelling on defining what is wrong and how it got that way, the solution-oriented therapist asks outcome questions, such as:

- If a miracle happened in your sleep tonight and solved all your problems, how would you be able to tell tomorrow that a miracle must have happened?
- How would your life be different if all your problems were solved?
- If you were living your life the way you wanted it and you made a movie, tell me what scenes I would see?

By focusing on solutions, the therapist can help the client define in specific terms how to achieve the desired goal or outcome without necessarily spending a great deal of time on the depressing details that led to the client's current situation. Brief-session therapists believe that even small changes will become amplified and lead to larger eventual changes. A therapist who wants to work from a solution orientation can do so with the treatment-resistant client and may find that the approach pays dividends and avoids the negativity of focusing on problems and pathology.

Develop a Treatment Plan

Most therapists find it helpful to develop an overview of the resistance a particular client seems to have. This overview can easily develop into a treatment plan. Using three sheets of paper, the counselor can identify the resistance to counseling, to change, and to the counselor. For example, the counselor lists on the first page in one column all the reasons the counselor suspects the client may be resisting counseling, such as fear of disclosure, cost, and so on. On the second page, the counselor lists the client's reasons for not wanting to change. This speculating does not need to be theory based but should be as specific as possible. For example, the counselor may write that the client does not want to change because he believes he does not have any problems or because he does not think changing would help his situation. On the third page, the counselor records the reasons the client may resist the counselor. For example, the counselor represents authority or coercion.

Having identified the client's resistance to counseling, change, and the counselor in a treatment plan, the counselor may try to empathize with this resistance, especially the resistance to change, by listing the disadvantages of not resisting. (Many counselors have difficulty with this exercise because it is counterintuitive, but it is very helpful.)

For example, for a person with an alcohol problem, the counselor should list some possible disadvantages of resisting or participating in the change process. First, the client would have to get new friends because all his old friends are drinking partners. Not only is this hard work but it is anxiety producing. Finding nondrinking friends requires new places to socialize and a whole new set of social activities. People who have never socialized without the benefit of alcohol often do not know how to stand, talk, mingle, and act when sober. A married client who has used alcohol to numb anger at a spouse might have to learn to deal with that anger or be at risk of expressing the anger in a dangerous way. The client might consider it safer to continue to drink than to be sober. At a minimum, the client would have to make some decisions about whether to remain in the relationship, and for most people, the thought of leaving a relationship, even a bad one, is distressing.

At a deeper level, a disadvantage of changing is that the client would have to develop a new self-concept as a person who does not drink. This is no small matter for someone who has oriented his life around the next drink and who has dealt with most emotions by numbing them with alcohol. Psychodynamic therapists conceptualize resistance as the stubborn persistence of the personality to satisfy basic drives.

Or, in newer psychodynamic theories (Weiss, 1993), psychotherapists postulate that resistance stems from the obstacles to changing one's basic dysfunctional beliefs about the world, even if the individual wishes to do so. Regardless of the theoretical frame of reference, it is possible for the counselor to see the inherent difficulty the client will face with change and empathize with the client's concerns.

Therapy with people with "bad habits" (smoking, for instance), unfortunately, often degenerates into the therapist imploring the client to stop. This, of course, does not work. Clients struggle against the counselor as they have against probably dozens of others who have attempted to change them. It is more effective to empathize with clients by identifying the reasons why they will have difficulty changing. This empathy helps the client feel understood, and, paradoxically, permits the client to embrace the possibility of change. If the counselor tells the client to change, the client answers by saying why it is not possible. If the counselor empathizes with the difficulties in the path of change, the client can focus on the need for change.

Paradoxical directives are sometimes effective for behaviorally defiant clients (Tennen et al., 1981; Frankl, 1960). For example, a client who is suspicious of a therapist might be encouraged to be especially careful and supported in his notion that it is important to be careful about trusting people until they are better known. However, paradoxical behavior directives have the potential to backfire, and they may rely too much on gimmicks for some therapists. For example, it is obviously dangerous to challenge a suicidal client to go ahead and jump. Empathy, on the other hand, is a commonly recognized core condition of effective therapy, and supreme empathy (taking empathy to its logical conclusion) is quite paradoxical by itself. When a counselor empathizes with the many reasons the client identifies for not being able to make a change, the client often begins to argue why change is necessary, after all, as the following example shows:

Counselor: I can see how difficult it would be for you to not be angry at your wife. If you didn't get mad, you're concerned that she would control everything in your relationship.

Client: Yeah, she does try to run my life. I'm not gonna put up with that.

Counselor: You feel you've got a right to be angry and threatening. You'd rather have her call the cops on you than have her call the shots.

Client: Yeah, but I don't want the cops in the middle of my life either.

Counselor: But you'd rather have the police come than feel controlled by your wife, and you can't find a way to work things out with your wife without getting angry.

Client: Yeah, but I need to do something.

Counselor: But how can you work things out and still feel like a man? You don't see any way to do that.

Client: Yeah, that's right. But if I don't do something, she'll leave me for good or I'll be in jail.

It seldom works out so easily with reluctant clients identifying what they need to do. Unfortunately, it is quite predictable that clients will defeat the therapist's attempts to identify the "right" course of action.

This chapter outlined several general principles for conducting therapy with difficult clients, irrespective of the counselor's theoretical frame of reference. These principles lead us to select a number of techniques that may be useful with the difficult client. Next, we examined the preliminary meeting of the counselor with a difficult client and suggested several tasks that should be accomplished.

Working with resistant clients can be frustrating but also can be fun because it is so challenging. It is important for counselors to have some ideas about how to respond to barriers to counseling created by clients. Otherwise, the counseling degenerates into lecturing and posturing, and no change can occur with the resulting polarization of participants.

REFERENCES

American Psychiatric Association. 1987. *Diagnostic and Statistical Manual, Vol. III* (Revised). Washington, D.C.: American Psychiatric Association.

_____. 1994. *Diagnostic and Statistical Manual, Vol. IV*. Washington, D.C.: American Psychiatric Association.

Anderson, C. and S. Stewart. 1983. *Mastering Resistance*. New York: Guilford Press.

Beck, A., F. Wright, C. Newman, and B. Liese. 1993. *Cognitive Therapy of Substance Abuse*. New York: Guildford Press.

Dowd, D. and F. Wallbrown. 1993. Motivational Components of Client Reactance. *Journal of Counseling and Development*. 71: 533-37.

Ellis, A. 1985. *Overcoming Resistance*. New York: Springer Publishing Company.

Enright, J. and R. Estep. 1973. Metered Counseling for the Reluctant Client. *Psychotherapy: Theory Research and Practice*. 10:305-7.

Erickson, M. 1980. Resistant Patient. In E. L. Rosse, ed. *The Nature of Hypnosis and Suggestion, Vol. 1*. New York: Irvington Publishers.

Frankl, V. 1960. Paradoxical Intention: A Logotherapeutic Technique. *American Journal of Psychotherapy*. 14:520-35.

Goodyear, R. K. and F. O. Bradley. 1980. The Helping Process as Contractual. *Personnel and Guidance Journal*. 58:512-15.

Korn, R. and L. McCorkle. 1959. *Criminology and Penology*. New York: Rinehart and Winston.

Lazarus, A. 1992. Multimodal Therapy. In J. C. Norcross and M. R. Goldfried, eds. *Handbook of Psychotherapy Integration*. New York: Basic Books.

Lazarus, A. and A. Fay. 1983. Resistance or Rationalization. In P. Wachtel, ed. *Resistance: Psychodynamic and Behavior Approaches*. New York: Plenum Press.

Meloy, R., A. Haroun, and E. Schiller. 1990. *Clinical Guidelines for Involuntary Outpatient Treatment*. Sarasota, Florida: Professional Resource Exchange.

Riordan, R. J., K. B. Matheny, and C. Harris. 1978. Helping Counselors Minimize Client Reluctance. *Counselor Education and Supervision*. 18(1): 14-22.

Rooney, R. 1992. *Strategies for Work with Involuntary Clients*. New York: Columbia University Press.

Samenow, S. 1984. *Inside the Criminal Mind*. New York: Times Books.

Selekman, M. 1993. *Pathways to Change: Brief Therapy Solutions with Difficult Adolescents*. New York: Guilford Press.

Strean, H. 1985. *Resolving Resistance in Psychotherapy*. New York: John Wiley.

Teismann, M. 1980. Convening Strategies in Family Therapy. *Family Progress*. 19:373-400.

Tennen, H., M. Rohrbaugh, S. Press, and L. White. 1981. Reactance Theory and Therapeutic Paradox: A Compliance/Defiance Model. *Psychotherapy: Theory, Research and Practice*. 18(1):14-22.

Watzlawick, P., J. Beavin, and D. Jackson. 1967. *Pragmatics of Human Communication*. New York: Norton.

Weiss, J. 1993. *How Psychotherapy Works*. New York: Guilford Press.

Yochelson, S. and S. Samenow. 1976. *The Criminal Personality: Profile for Change*. New York: Jason Aronson.

_____. 1977. *The Criminal Personality: The Change Process*. New York: Jason Aronson.

Young, M. E. 1992. *Counseling Methods and Techniques: An Eclectic Approach*. New York: Merrill.

CHAPTER

3

Clarifying the Therapist's Role

Pam Stanchfield

Corrections Program Therapist

Sex Offender Treatment Program

Lino Lakes Correctional Facility

Lino Lakes, Minnesota

in the Treatment of the Resistant Sex Offender

Although the maintenance of clear and appropriate boundaries is crucial to all thera-
peutic relationships, this is never more important than in the therapeutic relationship with
sex offender clients. The sex offender therapist must be able to encourage, challenge, and
confront clients while simultaneously preserving personal ethics and program integrity.
Clarifying the therapist's role is accomplished directly, through statements to the client, and
indirectly, through modeling. This chapter offers readers an array of methods for achieving
this clarity, and specific examples of countermeasures clients may use to undermine the
therapeutic relationship.

Therapeutic styles vary greatly. It is this author's belief that therapy in general, and sex offender therapy specifically, is both an art and a science. Recognizing when to apply what you know, and how to apply it to a given situation, takes skill, experience, and patience. Being able to understand where the clients are, how they are feeling now, what they might be thinking, and how they might be relating their current thoughts and feelings to experiences from their past, will assist the therapist in making decisions about which techniques to apply and when and how to apply them. This process allows the therapist to sense what the client's needs are at any given moment.

When the therapist does not know what the client is thinking or feeling, she or he needs to be able to assess what the client is most likely to be thinking and feeling. This chapter is written to be helpful for those who work with resistant sex offender clients. It describes how the author uses therapeutic interventions in a specific setting: an intensive, inpatient, long-term treatment program for incarcerated sex offenders. Therapists who work in other settings will need to modify these tools to fit their program needs and individual therapeutic styles.

Even within a specific treatment modality, the use of each of these tools needs to be adapted to the variety of therapeutic interactions available. For example, a psycho-educational class provides different opportunities than the group therapy environment, or an individual counseling session. Each clinician will need to develop a comfortable style that works for her or him, as it applies to each of these settings.

All of the tools have historic roots that have been combined and applied in a variety of ways that the author has found to be most useful in her experience working with incarcerated sex offenders. As you read this chapter, you will note many elements that are familiar from a broad variety of therapeutic perspectives. They include Salvador Minuchin's joining theory, Carl Rogers' stance of unconditional warm regard, elements of Irvin Yalom's existential therapy, a healthy portion of Albert Ellis' reality therapy, seasoned with Yochelson and Samenow's criminal thinking theory, and so forth. Although the techniques and therapeutic interventions are adapted from these theories, they may not work for you without your own modifications. They work for this author given her therapeutic style and approach to sex offender treatment.

In addition to using therapeutic tools that are comfortable, it is also important for therapists to be aware of their own emotions at all times, because they are often a key to what is going on with the client. The client is best served when therapists use their recognition of themselves as human beings to empathize with the client's perspective. Empathic awareness includes the ability and the desire to understand the nuances of the client's reality. It is human to have emotional reactions to things going on around us. It is crucial that therapists be able to counter the shame that clients bring with them to the process, by continuously reminding them of their humanness. Sex offenders often deny their own humanity and use the shame this produces to justify hurting others. Therapists can use their self-awareness to imagine what the client might be experiencing, while being careful not to confuse the client's emotions with their own.

Emotional confusion can be created during the development of the therapeutic relationship. It can be a very unsettling experience when a client directs behavior toward the therapist that normally would be perceived as socially unacceptable. This may occur when clients cross or attempt to cross the therapist's boundaries through overt or covert sexualizing of the relationship, or through graphic descriptions of the abuse and violence they have perpetrated on others. These are actions and disclosures that would ordinarily cause us to feel repelled. However, a therapist must be able to clarify his or her role in the relationship to be able to incorporate this otherwise repugnant information as a deepening of the therapeutic alliance.

It is also central to the therapeutic relationship that the therapist be able to see the irony of the high level of intimacy required for the relationship to be effective. Without the ability to sustain this ironic detachment at the same time as maintaining empathic awareness of the client's essential humanity, therapists are in danger of taking on the client's emotions as their own. Clinicians also must be alert to the danger of joining too closely with the client, thus mimicking a peer relationship, rather than maintaining a healthy therapeutic distance.

Information that clients supply during the course of an interaction can be used to assess and evaluate their core beliefs about relationships and power. This then can be reflected back to them. Such a reflection becomes useful to clients in learning to challenge themselves regarding their thinking and behavior. Both art and science must be employed in determining when specific tools are most effective. Readers are cautioned not to say or do anything with a client unless completely comfortable with the technique employed, including an understanding regarding how and why such techniques could be useful to this particular client, at this time.

The science of this work is in knowing the techniques, understanding their use, and applying them correctly. The art is about understanding the clients' likely thoughts and emotions at that moment and the possible thoughts and emotions that might be paired from their past experiences. The art also requires the practitioner to be able to imagine possible ways that clients might be distorting past and current reality, particularly their current emotional reality, and being able to reframe that for the clients in such a way that their current experience is validated. This allows the client to consider choosing to accept the need to challenge their current beliefs about their past, present, and future.

When practicing this art, therapists develop awareness of where the client is, within his or her body and mind. Pay close attention to the clients' body language, as well as the content of what they say. The therapist will occasionally ask the clients where they are, and where they have gone, what they are thinking about now, and what they are remembering from the past. The therapist as artist will make sure that clients stay in the present so the scientist can work with them there.

Anti-sex-offense Devices

Part of the art of treating sex offenders is reorienting the client to the past, present, or future as the encounter dictates. The author refers to these techniques as "anti-sex-offense devices" because they help the therapist avoid falling into the traps created by the client's presentation of reality, or "the truth" as he or she sees it. These techniques are called anti-sex-offense devices because they are countermaneuvers for certain ploys which sex offenders in treatment tend to repeat as a means of not taking responsibility for their choices. The anti-sex-offense devices described here include: the reframe refrain, the three v's, pep talks, and un-defocusing.

The Reframe Refrain

"I'm not calling you a liar, I'm telling you I don't believe you."

The reframe refrain is a continuous presentation of the truth as the therapist sees it in paradox to what the client experiences or tends to believe, about what is currently happening. The reframe refrain reflects the current truth, the most likely past truth, and the truth regarding possibilities for the future. It is a statement and a restatement about reality, minus the distortions that accompany the client's presentation and experience of the truth.

Sex offender therapists providing the client with a reframe refrain will often find the client in disagreement with them. The client will likely say something in the nature of, "Are you calling me a liar?" To this, the reply should be, "No, I am not calling you a liar. However, I am telling you one of the following things:

- I don't believe you.
- It is not believable.
- It defies logic.
- It is ludicrous.

The therapist can supply any appropriate response to suit the current situation. What is most important is paying attention to what the clients are saying, and responding to it using their language, while continuing to reframe it. This gives the clients a good dose of reality therapy, and they never can get enough of that. When the clients begin to consistently present reality without distortions, they can reframe for themselves. They should be encouraged to do this often and in all situations pertinent to their treatment.

It is important to keep in mind that you are dealing with the clients' experience of reality. This is their experience of the world. They may not be currently accessing the larger truth, absent their cognitive distortions. The therapist must find a way to validate their perceptions, while simultaneously reframing it as their perception, identifying possible distortions or having them identify possible distortions. To validate means to recognize and acknowledge that whatever the clients are presenting as the truth or reality is their experience of it.

It can best be comprehended by taking into account possible lenses through which the clients may view the world. It is probable that clients will be dishonest at times. If however, the clinician is fairly certain that the clients are presenting their honest perception, there are common distortions, which may color their view. The way they describe reality may be what they remember it to be, may be how they wished it to be, or may be how they want us to believe it was. Validating means accepting this as the clients' experience or belief. At the same time, the therapist must guide the clients to see that some of their thinking is likely to be distorted. Reframing involves clarifying reality.

Another ploy clients use to disagree with the therapist is the client question, "Don't you trust me?" The response to this should be an emphatic, "No!" "Don't you trust me?" is a trick question. It is one of the ways that perpetrators manipulate victims. Clients must learn that trust is not all-inclusive. Specify what you do and do not trust about them. Examples of statements one might say to the client are as follows: "I trust you will show up in time for group. I trust you will follow the directives of security staff. I trust you will behave appropriately in front of me. I trust you may behave differently when therapy staff are not present." To the last statement, a client may reply with some version of these questions, "What do you mean? Are you accusing me of something?"

The clinician should reply, "No, I am not accusing you of anything. I am saying that men in a prison treatment program sometimes behave differently, depending upon whether or not therapy staff are present. I am letting you know I understand this might be the case for you as well. Your behavior will demonstrate whether you behave differently when therapy staff are not present." The therapist could also say something like, "I am saying that someone who has behaved in such a way as to end up in a sex offender treatment program might behave one way when therapy staff are present and another way when therapy staff are not present." Do not be trapped into agreeing to the clients' perspective. They most likely will be persistent in their attempts to reframe your reality. Continue to reframe their reality until the clients can accurately reflect what you are saying.

Another common sex offender ploy is to say something to the effect of "You can't prove it." To this the therapist can reply, "I don't intend to prove anything. I am not going to attempt to prove anything. It is your job to demonstrate that you are doing the things you need to do, and that you are addressing your treatment goals. I will make the best clinically sound decisions I can make, based on the best information I have. Based on what I currently know or believe to be true, I am making this decision, in what I believe to be in your best interest."

The therapist also may reply "I have to make decisions no matter how much information I have. I don't always have the truth. Sometimes people in situations similar to your current situation are not completely honest with me. I am not saying you are lying. I am just saying I can understand that a man in your situation might lie." The therapist could also say "I don't know if you are lying or not. Only you really know that. I only know what I believe. You can't control what I believe. You can only control what you choose to say to me and what you choose to do. I can tell you what I believe or I can keep it to myself. If you want to know what I think, I may tell you. If I think you need to know, I will tell you."

There are many situations in an inpatient prison setting where a therapist must make a decision in the absence of clear and definite information. One of the situations that this author has run into regards the suspension of a client for something that he appears to be doing which is disruptive to the rest of the community. In those cases when he asks her to prove it, she may say "I am suspending you because I believe you have behaved inappropriately." To which the client likely will reply, "You can't prove it." In replying to him, she might say, "I do not intend to prove anything. I am not trying to prove anything. You need to demonstrate to me that you are meeting program expectations. It is up to you to demonstrate that. At this time, you are not demonstrating that clearly. I am making the best decision that I can. I am making this decision in your best interest."

It is important when "singing" the reframe refrain in an attempt to redirect the client's behavior and thinking (such as when warning or confronting) to emphasize that you are telling clients what they might do. The clinician knows and can help them to understand what they might do. The clinician does not know what they will do. Speculating upon potential future abusive behavior is an important therapeutic task. Words used and tone of voice is always critically important. The client should not be told that they *will* do something. Emphasizing *will* can negatively influence clients, as it telegraphs inevitably. Clients need to hear that past behavior is not always a predictor of future behavior. Past behavior can be a reminder that they can and must choose how they think and behave.

The Three V's

The three v's are: Validate, Validate, Validate. A therapist cannot validate sex offenders' reality and experience too often if the therapist wants to join successfully with the clients. Once the therapeutic relationships have been established through validation, the clients are more likely to reveal what is truly going on with them.

Additionally, clients may reveal their understanding of reality; why they think about things the way they do and why they feel the way they do. This allows the therapist to move into the realm of helping the client to challenge themselves regarding their current core beliefs, distorted thoughts, and unhealthy expression of emotions. The clients then can develop healthier core beliefs about the world, which can positively influence their thoughts and the expression of their emotions.

There are many things that a therapist must validate for clients consistently throughout the course of their interactions. Validate the clients' attractions. They currently may experience inappropriate attraction and arousal. The clients' attraction and arousal to inappropriate sexual partners may continue after treatment, and may be something that the clients will be faced with for the rest of their lives. It is very important not to miss this element. Validate that this is who or what their current attractions are. Attempts to talk clients out of their attractions only lessen the clinician's effectiveness, because the clients will not be able to relate to what the therapist is saying. An understanding of attraction and arousal is key for the clients' development of proper and appropriate interventions for their sexual assault cycle.

Validate the clients' perceptions. Validate their distortions, underscoring that they are distortions. They are what the clients have believed, thought, or felt. Validate the clients' emotions and self-talk. The clients' self-talk will lead them into healthy or unhealthy decisions. It is crucial in sex offender therapy that the clients' self-talk become healthy. Validate the notion of choice in general. Behavior is one choice that is always available to them. Validate that a particular behavior is only one of many choices that the clients have, that the locus of control for choice resides within them. Validate that it is their dilemma, that sex offender treatment is their treatment. What happens to them is their experience. Validate what their past experiences might have been like. Validate fears they may have about the future and hurtful and frightening emotions they may have from their past.

If clients tell you in the course of treatment, "It's not fair," or "Life's not fair," or something else is not fair, be sure to validate that they are correct. "It's not fair!" is one of the most important things to validate for a sex offender. It is a part of criminal thinking to justify inappropriate behavior by claiming that one thing or another was not fair. Validate where the client is at the present and may always be. It is difficult to choose healthy behavior given unhealthy attractions. Validate, and acknowledge the truth of it, when they say something like "You don't know what it's like," or "You haven't had these things happen to you."

Acknowledge to them that you may not have done, or had done to you, the events that they have experienced. Stress, however, that you have experienced hurt, anger, pain, loneliness, disappointment, dread, powerlessness, and sadness. Say, "I, too, have been angry and confused. I, the human, have had pain. I, the human, know what it feels like to hurt. What hurts me and what hurts you is unique. I struggle and always will. All humans struggle in their own way."

When speaking to a client, the author talks about emotions without the details of personal events, which could leave her vulnerable. She talks about the philosophy of events. "I know what it's like to be a parent. I know what it feels like to experience a loss." In joining, we sometimes misread a client and can cause shame or leave ourselves vulnerable. If we see our clients as human beings first, we can join them there. There is always an in.

When a client says, "It is hard," validate that. Say, "Yes it is. It is hard. Life is very hard." When a client says to the author, "You don't know what it's like," she tells him, "You're right, I don't" or "I'm sure I don't" or "Probably not." She may say to him, "I can imagine" or "I am sure" or "I can imagine it was" or "I'm sure it would be awful, (terrible, horrible, devastating, traumatic, life-changing, and so forth)." She may say, "I don't know everything about it, but I do know it would be awful (horrible, terrible, devastating, and so forth)." She may say, "So tell me how it feels, because I don't know."

Clients need to know that they are not alone. Other people have felt like they feel. There is a way that they can feel okay. The therapist might say to him, "If it happened to me, it would be very difficult, challenging, disheartening, discouraging, or frightening."

Clarifying for the Client

When working with a client, there is a tendency to answer any questions that the client may pose. Keep in mind that the role of the therapist is one of clarifying information for the client as opposed to providing answers for the client. The author often tells clients that it is her job to make sure that they ask the right questions, not to supply answers for them, that she is there to help them understand what questions they need to ask themselves or others.

It is the therapist's role to assist in the journey, to point out roads along the way. Let the clients know that some of the roads they may choose are roads to nowhere. Other roads that they may be able to identify, or that you may point out to them, are roads to somewhere. Help them to clarify in which direction they are headed. While you are singing the reframe refrain and clarifying their perceptions of reality, they will need feedback about their choices and other options that would be healthier for them.

One of the questions to ask them is, "Where do you want to go?" Then, help them work backwards from their goal to discover how to get there. It is part of the therapist's job to continuously validate what road the clients are on, and to help them understand where they want to go and how to get there. It is all a part of the same task that you do all along, to validate and reframe simultaneously.

Pep Talks

Since sex offender treatment is an art and a science, a therapist must be ready to identify and respond to clients' needs to hold a belief that they can "make it out there" and that they can attain a sense of belonging. It is not always necessary or appropriate to confront the sex offenders' thinking and behavior in a critical way. What is the purpose of tearing down their crumbling walls of distorted thinking and abusive behavior if the walls are not going to be rebuilt by bricks of caring behavior, held together by the mortar of rational thinking? Many clients will benefit from a periodic pep talk that encourages them to "be about something."

At these times, therapists should be full of enthusiasm for life, reflecting their hope for a better world and their belief in possibilities and personal growth. Approach clients as a teacher, coach, or loving parent might, wanting the best for them. Be filled with hope. These clients have too few opportunities to experience moments of unqualified hope for them as viable members of society; or to experience others' belief that they have the ability and the desire to make healthy choices, which will impact them and their loved ones in positive ways. Not unlike teaching persons to fish rather than providing them with fish, therapists can teach clients to have faith that they can succeed, so that they will be more likely to decide to make the kinds of choices which will lead to success. This is also a way to relate behavior and thinking to a healthy cycle, where some of the elements previously used for unhealthy purposes (such as fantasy and planning) can be used to "practice" and reinforce healthy behavior and thinking.

Moments of unqualified hope must include hope for the clients as individuals as well as hope for them as individuals who have committed a sex offense. Emphasize that your belief in them and hope for them comes from the knowledge that they can and will choose how they behave and how they think. They have all the choices, every day, all the time. Do not be afraid to tell them that. Consistently remind them, "You can choose. You have all the choices. You will choose. You can choose every day. You will choose every day. You can choose every minute. You will choose every minute. The choices you make determine who you are. They determine who you will be. The choices you make determine what kind of person you are. They determine what kind of person you will be. The choices you make demonstrate how you choose to treat others. The choices you make will influence how others choose to treat you. Your choices scream out your values. They are yours to make all day, every day, for the rest of your life."

Un-defocusing

The final anti-sex-offender device is called un-defocusing. Defocusing is a common trait of the sex offender client. Defocusing includes a variety of techniques employed by offenders to change the focus from the subject at hand, whether the subject is one of their sex offender treatment goals or attention to their behavior or thinking. Un-defocusing is a continuous refocus to the issue at hand.

For instance, when clients attempt to blame others for their own feelings, thoughts, or behaviors, one of the things the therapist can say to them is "That is your choice. Your choices are resulting in the consequences you are experiencing." During those opportunities when you want to join clients, you can ask them, "What do you want? I probably want what you want."

Help them brainstorm the things that they want in life. When the therapist is done brainstorming with clients, what will most likely be discovered is that the clients want personal growth, the ability to view themselves as safe persons, and financial security. They want to be of value to themselves and the community. You can further join them with the rest of the world by letting them know that this is what most people want, and these are important things to want and to have as goals.

A healthy vision of the future is an important part of sex offender treatment. Sex offenders need to be able to visualize a healthy future if they are going to live a healthy future. Talk about future behavior at the same time as past and present behavior. Talk about the kind of thinking that leads to healthy future behavior. The therapist always has to be mindful of future behavior because an integral part of the sex offender's treatment is personal growth. Personal growth is closely linked to a client's ability to self-challenge.

When providing sex offender therapy, you always need to be very direct and clear with clients. After ascertaining what they want, give them a reality check at the same time. Tell them, "I know how to help you get there. You don't know how to get there. If you knew how to get there, you would be there. Your way got you here." This should not be said in a shaming way, simply in a matter-of-fact way. Then, go ahead and talk about how to get the things that they want.

With regard to un-defocusing, it is imperative to stress that the therapeutic relationship is one where the therapist gets involved in the client's personal business. It is a not a two-way relationship by any means. That must be clarified and reclarified many times throughout the course of treatment. It is very simply stated, "That is not the nature of the relationship. It is not two-sided. It is not an equal partnership. It is a different kind of relationship."

Another ploy needing un-defocusing surfaces when the client gets into an argument with the therapist. The argument can be about anything. When the argument inevitably turns to the therapist's performance of duties, the client will often cite examples of unfairness or practitioner ineptitude. Use this as an opportunity to clarify the client's choices. Respond by saying, "We are not talking about my performance. We are talking about your choices and your behavior. You need to do something about it. I will be here tomorrow, I don't know if you will choose to be."

Continuously redirect and refocus clients to their treatment. Remind them that they are in treatment and you are not. It is your job to direct them and guide them. Say things in a nonshaming and direct way, maintaining eye contact. Clinicians can say the following when a client is being inappropriate in a conversation: "You work for me, I don't work for you." Sex offenders understand power. Since they understand hierarchies, make the boundaries very clear to them at all times.

In sex offender treatment, the therapist must decide the course of action. This often stimulates the client to decide to argue about something and accuse the therapist of making all the decisions. Again, this gives the therapist an opportunity to agree with the client, which is always a good idea. Tell the client, "I decide. It is okay if you don't understand the why of it."

Clients may not be able to understand why the therapist wants them to do something. That is okay. The author discourages clinicians from working too hard to insure that the clients understand why the therapist wants them to do something. It is not always important that the clients understand why a task is being required, requested, or suggested. It is important that the clients understand what the therapist wants and expects them to do. Tell the client, "I decide. It is okay if you don't understand why I want you to do this," or "It is important that you understand what I want you to do."

Many sex offender clients are outwardly compliant. This, too, can be a form of resistance. If it is obvious that they are merely being compliant, and not really doing the work that they need to do to address their goal, let the clients know that compliance is not sufficient for the task at hand. They may try to argue that and say, "But I am doing what you want me to do." To this you can reply, "I determine your progress. It is up to me to assess that you are doing what you need to do. It is your job to demonstrate that you are doing what you need to do." Always turn their responsibilities back to them in the process of reframing and validating. You are validating that you are the one deciding those things. You do not need to argue with them. You need to keep reminding them that you are the measuring device.

The most resistant form of un-defocusing occurs when clients deliberately obfuscate, in which case, immediately cease all explanations. Then, ask the clients to explain in detail what they have heard about the expectations. Focus on the expectations until they can reflect them back to you accurately. In dealing with resistance, the therapist has to remember that part of what clients need to do is save face. Take the resistance as it is and validate it, which is letting the client save face, and then they can go ahead and make healthier choices.

Working with sex offenders is both trying and interesting. Maintaining healthy therapeutic boundaries is essential to providing treatment for this resistant and unusually manipulative clientele. Therapists can artfully administer the science involved in the practice of sex offender therapy. They can seize opportunities to use the truth to expose reality. By revealing the truth to their clients and helping them challenge distorted thinking, clinicians can guide clients to honestly take responsibility for their actions. This therapeutic relationship provides a safe environment for clients to explore their choices and understand how they impact others. Viewing all others as worthy of compassion, and finding ways to care about those who are hard to care for, helps all of us to maintain our own humanity.

REFERENCES

Ellis, A. 1985. *Overcoming Resistance*. New York: W. W. Norton.

Minuchin, S. 1974. *Families and Family Therapy*. Cambridge, Massachusetts: Harvard University Press.

Rogers, C. R. 1951. *Client-centered Therapy*. Boston: Houghton Mifflin.

Stanchfield, Pam. *Zen and the Art of Sex Offender Therapy*. Unpublished manuscript.

Yalom, I. D. 1980. *Existential Psychotherapy*. New York: Basic Books.

Yochelson, S. and S. Samenow. 1976. *The Criminal Personality: Profile for Change*. New York: Jason Aronson.

CHAPTER 4

Some Practical Methods

Jerry Larke
Psychologist
Marshfield, Massachusetts

of Treating the Mandated Client

Reprinted from Psychotherapy 22(2):262-268 (1990) with some minor modifications. Used by permission.

Each therapist must develop an extensive array of tactics for responding to the mandated client's resistance to the change process and the development of an appropriate therapeutic relationship. Methods used will need to be mindful of the characteristics that the mandated client is likely to display, and the responses that the therapist is likely to experience as a result of client cynicism and mistrust. The level of resistance encountered in their incarcerated clients frequently dismays clinicians entering the field of corrections, and helpers with many years of encountering such resistance can experience difficulty with creatively engaging with yet another recalcitrant client. This chapter offers an overview of strategies for engagement with this difficult client population.

Pressure from an increasing number of societal concerns has resulted in the establishment of programs to identify and treat the sex offender, the child abuser, the alcohol and substance abuser, and others involved in the criminal justice system. These so-called "resistant clients" are seldom included in the typical mental health caseload. In fact, the absence of effective treatment methods and notoriously poor therapeutic outcomes are well documented (Goldstein, 1973; Schofield, 1964). Paradoxically, as more of these individuals are identified and mandated, or forced into accepting mental health treatment, there are extremely few mental health facilities or private practitioners available. The mental health practitioner has either little desire or feels inadequately trained to serve individuals with lifestyle problems. To compound the problem further, traditional mental health workers are taught that, for effective treatment to occur, clients must become involved of their own free will and be "internally motivated to change" through their own efforts.

This chapter presents some experience-based, practical methods of treating the compulsory client with an array of alternative methods targeted toward this population. Despite the commonly held view that psychotherapy is primarily a middle- and upper-class activity, there exists ample evidence of attempts to modify treatment for the unmotivated client.

In the area of family therapy, Salvadore Minuchin and his associates (1974) have focused on the therapy needs of inner-city minority clients. Goldstein (1973) developed structured learning therapy, a behavioral skill building approach, as psychotherapy for the poor. Anthony (1980) recommended teaching a repertoire of skills to enable the so-called rehabilitative or chronic client to cope more independently.

Pepper (1982) reported on an innovative mental health program tailored to reach the young adult chronic client, a new group of "uninstitionalized" clients, who typically resist treatment until forced or coerced by legal authorities. Based on his experience, Pepper prefers that the young adult chronic clients be on probation or referred as an alternative to jail, so more social controls and expectations can be placed on them.

An addition to the mental healthcare delivery system, the case manager, functions as informal therapist and often uses this relationship to entice resistant or noncompliant clients into appropriate treatment (Lamb, 1980). Nontraditional clinics, such as walk-in centers, also have been used to attract the reluctant client into continuing drug maintenance (Anthony, 1980). Van Putten (1982) suggested the direct teaching of the importance of compliance in chemotherapy with psychiatric clients.

However, the majority of literature citations deal with the obvious dilemmas of involuntary inpatient hospitalization (Dunham, 1971; Liss and Allen, 1975) and forced treatment of aggressive clients (Madden, 1977). Except for case-specific psychoanalytic treatment (for example, Bell and Hobb, 1971), minimal literature exists on outpatient treatment of sex offenders.

The bulk of studies involving compulsory treatment are found in the alcohol and substance abuse literature. The predominant finding seems to be that there exists little or no difference between mandated or voluntary clients vis-a-vis success at modifying alcohol use (Laundergan et al., 1979). In fact, some have found recidivism rates to be lower with the mandated population (Ward and Allivane, 1979; Latessa, 1999). These studies expose the "motivational myth" that voluntary clients appear at the outset to be desirous of treatment but tend to drop out when symptoms are reduced (marriage stability, regaining temper control, and so forth). In contrast, the mandated client is forced to persist and ultimately may learn to be less fearful and resistant to treatment. Holser (1980) reported that in the case of alcoholic clients, while in the process of getting their driver's license returned, a significant number became highly motivated to remain in treatment.

Likewise, Dunham and Mauss (1982) reported that coercive referral rendered successful treatment outcome considerably more likely than did the voluntary self-referral. There also is some evidence that court-referred clients without an adjudication date are more resistant, violent, and poorer candidates than those with a hearing date. As a result, Rinella (1976) and Garrett (1981) recommended that only serious alcohol problems be mandated to intensive treatment, while less serious abusers be enrolled in educational programs. McGuire (1981) has studied the effectiveness of several drinking-driver programs and concluded that intensive and possibly long-term treatment be given the heavy abuser and less expensive countermeasures be developed for the light drinker.

Ten-year follow-up studies of compulsory treatment after driving while intoxicated (DWI) convictions in California by Reis (1980, 1981) revealed that the length of time in treatment was predictive of lowered recidivism rates; that is, treatment of at least one year or more was associated with permanent change. Other studies (Egerston et al., 1997; Gerstein and Harwood, 1990; and McLellan et al., 1997) have substantiated the importance of matching length of stay to clients' drug of choice and potential for relapse/recidivism.

In Western Europe there appears to be a greater tendency than in the United States to force criminal justice offenders, alcoholics, and sex offenders into treatment. Several authors contend successful outcome for such policies (Beltran-Ballester, 1979; Milosavcevic,1975). On the other hand, Norway seems to be decreasing in its reliance on mandated treatment while that country's suicide rate for the drug and alcohol abuser has risen. Nyhus (1979) draws a direct relationship between these two events. Arbor et al. (1976) and Polick et al. (1980) in a review of alcohol treatment outcome studies concluded: (1) a majority of clients improved in life functioning as a result of treatment; (2) different types of treatment (individual, group, and so forth) had no differential effects; but (3) treatment amount is the only variable having a significant effect on outcome.

Assumptions about Treatment

The following are some useful assumptions that can assist the therapist in treating the compulsory client.

1. **Focused motivation.** Motivation for treatment does exist in the compulsory client although sometimes it is vague, compartmentalized, or unavailable. It is multifaceted and differentially reinforced. "Motivation for what?" is the relevant question. The client may well be motivated to work on the return of his or her driver's license, completion of probation, or to receive a positive report to family court. In short, identify the referent and motivation may be possible.

2. **Application of the borderline/narcissistic personality-disorder material.** The contribution of Kohut (1971, 1977) and Masterson (1982) seem especially useful with this population. (For an excellent review *see* Campbell,

1982.) Many mandated clients are fixated at a primitive level much like the borderline and typically use seven primitive defenses of (1) avoidance, (2) acting-out, (3) denial, (4) clinging, (5) splitting, (6) projective identification, and (7) projection. Also, one or more of the four ego effects may exist: low frustration tolerance, poor impulse control, poor ego functioning, and diffuse ego boundaries.

3. **Awareness of fragile self-image.** Underlying a tough external shell exists a fragile self-image amenable to validation and acceptance by the therapist, which enables the client to experience the self apart from the parent, spouse, or bottle. The result is the experiencing of the evolving self in a more independent, capable, and self-sufficient manner.

4. **Value of therapy.** In the context of compulsory treatment, psychotherapy is viewed as a seduction process with the goal being long-term treatment and follow-up care. The general strategy involves confronting the primitive defenses, validating the experience of the person, and focusing on separation/individuation issues. Equally important is the acquisition of concrete observable skills and the modeling of a quality relationship which may enable the client to overcome his or her fears of intimacy and closeness in an interpersonal relationship.

5. **Use of adjuncts.** The positive impact of traditional office therapy can be enhanced by the use of adjuncts to treatment (for example, self-help groups such as Alcoholics Anonymous, Parents Anonymous, Recover Inc., church, and other informal social support systems). See Read, *Partners in Change: The 12-Step Referral Handbook for Probation, Parole and Community Corrections* (1996) for useful guidelines for such referrals.

6. **Use of multimodel approach.** The use of a multimodel approach using behavioral contracting, the teaching of practical skill, and employing homework seems most appropriate (Cautella,1980; Sheldon and Ackerman,1976). The focus of treatment should be on increasing insight. An experiential knowledge of the culture of jails, prisons, and other institutions also would be helpful to the therapist. An open and frank review of the therapist's relevant work history can enhance competence with the skeptical client.

Alternative Treatment Methods

Especially important to successful treatment of the mandated client is the establishment of clear, simple referral procedures. When the mental health worker decides to accept the mandated client for treatment, several critical ethical issues must be clarified. As Chafetz (1965) said, if we are to protect the rights of the individual, compulsory treatment ought to be just one more technique in the caretaker's list of tools for enhancing motivation and needs we assume to exist in these clients. Fagan and Fagan (1982) speak of differentiating between a court referral and the legal coercion to keep the client in treatment. The task of the therapist is to maximize the quality of the referral by educating the referral source (the probation officer, lawyer, child-abuse worker, and so forth) in the importance of administering treatment at a time when a person seems remorseful, depressed, or is verbalizing a desire to understand something about himself or herself. Within the legal system, myths about mental health treatment are usually present. The therapist must help the referring agent have realistic expectations of treatment. It is important to explain that treatment is not punishment, nor should referrals be made in frustration or as a desperate maneuver.

Of course, frequency and duration of treatment, the estimated cost, and how it is to be paid, common procedures used, and typical interim goals must be reviewed. The referral source needs to understand and support the concept that long-term treatment represents a viable alternative to deterrence methods and recidivism.

Behavioral Contracting and Time-limited Therapy

The benefits of behavioral contracting with the psychotherapy client are well known. However, to the mandated client, behavioral contracting forms the essential cornerstone of treatment. At the first meeting, there is an attempt made to set the atmosphere of subsequent meetings by modeling honesty, openness, directness, and respect. The client is told that the medical record has not been read in advance so as to avoid prejudice and preconceived opinions.

The following items of confidentiality are stressed:

1. All contacts from others must have prior approval of the client at each contact. This would include employer, family member, judge, and lawyer, and

whether the client signed a release or not. Explain that only a court of record legally can request the medical record. Clients get copies of all reports to courts, lawyers, judges, and so forth.

2. At each session, all contacts of the previous week are discussed.

3. Offer to review the medical record and case notes with the client to establish trust.

4. Finally, stress the importance of independence and distance from the referral source and the role of therapist as a helper of individuals and as a person who can help them to avoid or prevent future problems.

Next, formulate treatment goals to establish the purpose for meeting. Mandated clients often establish such goals as regaining custody of their children, successfully completing parole, or securing a positive recommendation for return of a driver's license. As a potent incentive, positive reports are sent to the legal authorities documenting client consistency (such as keeping appointments, completing homework assignments, attending AA, or Parents Anonymous meetings). The majority of behavioral interventions used are from Cautella (1980), Sheldon and Ackerman (1976), and Wallace (1978). Treatment plans then are signed by both the client and the therapist, and reviewed at regular intervals.

At session one, the expectations of client and therapist are set establishing the appointment time. To model consistency and reliability, the therapist should establish an inflexible, scheduled appointment time. This is especially important in establishing a relationship with clients whose parental figures were unreliable. The process of cancellation and the consequences of missed meetings are reviewed. Usually after the first missed meeting, the client is confronted by telephone. If the second meeting is missed, the client is forced to wait and resume treatment after others on the waiting list have begun. The referral source is informed after the second delinquency. Frequency and duration of treatment are established, usually weekly in the beginning, and for nine months to one year in duration. Review of cost and method of payment is done at this time.

The gathering of an in-depth social history allows the client to begin verbal ventilation of past unpleasant events, and the therapist encourages ventilation about the frustrations of coping with the pressures of life. Some special issues to explore are the failure of past treatment attempts, relationship failures, the client's view of the arrest record, work history and training, and the relationship of drug and/or alcohol abuse to antisocial behavior.

Time-limited therapy offers many advantages to the mandated client. After a thorough discussion of the benefits and liabilities of long-term treatment, the client often will settle down and accept, even if in a passive compliant manner, the course of treatment. Since many display impaired ego functioning (low frustration tolerance and poor impulse control, particularly), the setting of a termination date can help them learn patience and tolerance. Another hidden benefit of long-term time-limited therapy is the trying out of a new role, much in the spirit of Kelly's (1955) fixed-role therapy. Due to the length of time in the new role, the client may learn to feel some ownership and identity with this new set of behaviors. An example would be the problem drinker abstaining from alcohol, or the child abuser enrolling in a developmental psychology course and writing weekly reports on his or her experiences. This "artificial" transformation may provide sufficient dissonance for the client to begin working through the resistance to trying out a new identity.

Application of Kohut's Self-psychology and Masterson's Borderline Conditions Approaches

Overlooking the theoretical inconsistencies and disagreements within the borderline conditions literature, one readily can adapt many of these methods to treatment of the mandated client. Psychodynamically, many persons who comprise the mandated client category are viewed as being primitively fixated in diffuse ego boundaries and poor impulse control. Both Kohut and Masterson believe the establishment of a trusting relationship is the key to facilitating change.

Masterson believes the borderline triad of separation/individuation failure produces an abandonment depression, which is primitively defended. The therapeutic task is to confront the primitive defenses when they occur, causing the person to experience this abandonment depression and begin the working-through process of understanding his or her process of individuation. Masterson has revised his work to recommend two types of treatment—confrontive/supportive and reconstructive. Confrontive/supportive therapy is the treatment of choice for people who are unable, or are in too much pain, to work through their fixations and must adapt to society and function realistically.

Kohut (1971, 1977), on the other hand, recommends that the therapist validate the individual's dilemma or frustrations with life, thereby regulating the client's self-esteem. The therapist is to show great empathy for the plight of the person. This narcissistic entitlement provides a positive atmosphere for the person to explore the hurt and anger of often being downtrodden by society—family friends, fellow workers, and social agencies. The quest here is to mutually search and discover the positive or good self and help the person internalize this image along with the negative self which forms an integrated whole.

The therapist can encourage the ventilation of negative feelings and help the client release anger and rage. This basic orientation works well with mandated clients since in their environment, few people are often sympathetic or understanding. The therapist is a contrast to the more punitively oriented legal authorities and can encourage the client's rejection of the social stigma associated with the act or crime. From experience, one can assume that no one cherishes the stigma of society's outcasts: sex offenders, criminals, or substance abusers. It also can be assumed that the client desires to shed this negative self-image if only he or she knows how. An open discussion of the point usually is productive. Therapy sessions can function to successfully regulate the client's self-esteem around this important issue.

Family Therapy with One Person

Another practical method that can favorably affect mandated clients is the use of family therapy with the identified client (Bowen, 1978). Often the resistant client will not bring the spouse/girlfriend/boyfriend into treatment even though it was agreed upon at the outset. A common angry attitude expressed is, "It's my problem, so I'll pay for it. It doesn't, involve her." Rather than engage in a power struggle, the therapist may choose to teach the client to relate better with the spouse or other family members by assigning relationship tasks to be completed by the client between sessions. A client, for example, might decide to talk to his or her parents about their marriage.

Then, client and therapist are free to explore such questions as: What is the attitude of the mate toward the offense or toward the client? Has there been an increase in family tension? In spite of the generally accepted family therapy tenet of the importance of involving the mate in treatment, the therapist may find it more productive to work with each mate separately and avoid a mutually denying or resisting couple.

Use of Peer Support Groups

The potency of peer support or self-help groups is well known. However, the historical problems between professional mental health workers and self-help groups such as Alcoholics Anonymous and Recovery, Inc., are also known (Zimberg et al., 1978). Katz and Ralde (1981) studied "treatment packages" where traditional psychotherapy and alternative self-help groups were employed simultaneously, sequentially, or in alternation. Some clients transformed the apparent conflict into complementary and mutually enhancing help from different nonoverlapping sources. In the experience of the author, it is possible to work out positive and independent areas of clinical responsibility. For example, attendance at AA would assist the client with his or her drinking problem, freeing up the therapist to focus attention on separation/individuation issues and life-functioning concerns. Since many of these individuals are socially isolated, they receive little opportunity for companionship—or "twinship" in Kohut's terminology—and the discovery that they are not alone in this plight.

The client also has the opportunity to observe positive social models similar to himself or herself who have been successful in changing targeted behaviors, made progress in their legal difficulties, and acquired more positive attitudes toward their lives. Of course, the therapist has the obligation to be very knowledgeable about the self-help groups that his or her clients have been asked to attend. Only through the therapy relationship can the therapist be assured that the client is learning and progressing, as formal referrals cannot be made to self-help groups.

In the last three months of treatment, meetings usually are held monthly and are referred to as "aftercare" sessions. The focus is on (1) a discussion of homework assignments (pleasant events forms, self-control monitoring sheets, and so forth), (2) report of regular attendance at peer support groups, and (3) a review of personal and family gains (a vacation, a savings account, a remodeled room, better use of leisure time, social contacts, and so forth). During these last meetings, the spouse/girlfriend/boyfriend is asked to be involved to enhance learning transfer and reinforce persistence.

Special Treatment Issues

To successfully treat the mandated client, an array of therapist-specific issues must be considered. The therapist's role must be active and not passive. Mandated clients need a reality ego and real objects to guide them successfully through "new" social situations rather than resorting to old counterproductive, antisocial solutions. Also, the submissive therapist's failure to confront leads clients to feel that the therapist does not care. In fact, clients may feel that the therapist is dependent, needs approval, and fears the client's tendency to act out. The denigration of the therapist's potency must be resisted at all costs, keeping in mind that the borderline and many mandated clients see the therapist as the "enemy" and as a convenient scapegoat. (*See* Masterson [1982] for a comprehensive discussion of this point.) Another important contributor to the therapist's self-denigration is capitulating to the pressures of the client. Such an example would be to modify the treatment contract significantly by ending treatment early or prematurely allowing for the approval for the return of a driver's license.

To work successfully with this population, the therapist must combat the tendency to consciously or unconsciously give up on the therapeutic relationship. The actual presentation of the client's personality—which is often hostile, angry, unappreciative, or manipulative—provides ample justification or unconscious motivation to discontinue treatment. However, the therapist needs to recall the probable primitive fixation of these clients and refocus his or her attention on positive, observable gains to save the relationship from self-destruction.

Finally, the therapist must devote ample time to planning the intervention strategy for each resistant client. Regular clinical case consultation or peer supervision is helpful because the loss of objectivity is especially predictable. The therapist must be flexible in the treatment approach and be prepared to change direction if and when needed.

REFERENCES

Anthony, W. A. 1980. *The Principles of Psychiatric Rehabilitation.* Baltimore: University Park Press.

Arbor, D. J., J. M. Polick, and H. B. Stanbul. 1976. *Alcohol and Treatment.* Santa Monica, California: Rand Corporation.

Bell, A. P. and C. S. Hobb. 1971. *The Personality of a Child Molester.* Chicago: Aldine.

Beltran-Ballester, E. 1979. Drugs and the Penal Law. *Drug Alcohol.* 4:169-183.

Bowen, M. 1978. *Family Therapy in Clinical Practice.* New York: Jason Aronson.

Campbell, K. 1982. The Psychotherapy Relationship with Borderline Personality Disorders. *Psychotherapy: Theory, Research and Practice.* 19(2):166-193.

Cautella, J. R. 1980. *Behavioral Analysis: Form for Clinical Intervention. Vol. I.* Champaign, Illinois: Research Press.

Chafetz, M. E. 1965. Is Compulsory Treatment of the Alcoholic Effective? *Northwest Medicine.* 64:932-937.

Dunham, H. W. 1971. Legalized Compulsory Treatment for Psychiatric Illness. *American Journal of Public Health.* 61(6):1076-1079.

Dunham, R. G. and A. L. Mauss. 1982. Reluctant Referrals: The Effectiveness of Legal Coercion in Outpatient Treatment for Public Drinkers. *Journal of Drug Issues.* 12(1):5-20.

Egerston, J. A., D. M. Fox, and A. I. Leshner, eds. 1997. *Treating Drug Abusers Effectively.* Cambridge, Massachusetts: Blackwell Publishers of North America.

Fagan, R. W. and N. M. Fagan. 1982. Impact of Legal Coercion on the Treatment of Alcoholism. *Journal of Drug Issues.* 12(1):103-117.

Garrett, J. A. 1981. Adjustment Demand: Resistance to Alcoholism Treatment with DWI Population. In L. Goldberg, ed. *Drugs and Traffic Safety, Vol. III.* pp. 1429-1445.

Gerstein, D. R. and H. J. Harwood, eds. 1990. *Treating Drug Problems: Vol 1.* A Study of the Evolution, Effectiveness, and Financing of Public and Private Drug Treatment Systems (Committee for the Substance Abuse Coverage Study Division of Health Care Services, Institute of Medicine). Washington, D.C.: National Academy Press.

Goldstein, A. P. 1973. *Structured Learning Therapy: Towards Psychotherapy for the Poor.* New York: Academic.

Holser, M. A. 1980. *Motivational Myths, the Mandated Client and the Volunteer: A Comparison of Alcohol Programs for Mandated Clients and Volunteer Clients—An Opinion Survey.* Eugene, Oregon: Lane County Council of Alcoholism.

Katz, R. and E. Ralde. 1981. Community Alternatives to Psychotherapy. *Psychotherapy: Theory, Research and Practice.* 18(3):365-374.

Kelly, G. 1955. *The Psychology of Personal Constructs.* New York: W. W. Norton.

Kohut, H. 1971. *The Analysis of the Self.* New York: International Universities Press.

_____. 1977. *The Restoration of the Self.* New York: International Universities Press.

Lamb, H. R. 1980. Therapist Case Managers: More than Brokers of Service. *Hospital and Community Psychiatry.* 31:762764.

Latessa, Edward J., ed. 1999. *What Works: Strategic Solutions: The International Community Corrections Association Examines Substance Abuse*. Lanham, Maryland: International Community Corrections Association and American Correctional Association.

Laundegan, J. C., J. W. Spicer, and N. L. Krammerer. 1979. *Are Court Referrals Effective?* Center City, Minnesota: Hazleden Foundation.

Liss, R. and F. A. Allen. 1975. Court Mandated Treatment: Dilemmas for Hospital Psychiatry. *American Journal of Psychiatry*. 132(9):924-927.

Madden, D. J. 1977. Voluntary and Involuntary Treatment of Aggressive Patients. *American Journal of Psychiatry*. 124(5):553-555.

Masterson, J. F. 1982. *The Narcissistic and Borderline Disorders*. New York: Brunner/Mazel.

McGuire, F. L. 1981. Social Action and the Current State of Knowledge in Treating Drinking Drivers. *Abstracts and Reviews in Alcohol and Driving*. 2(1):11-13.

McLellan, A. T., G. R. Grissom, Zanis, D., Randall, M., Brill, P., and O'Brien, C. P. 1997. Problem-service "Matching" in Addiction Treatment: A Prospective Study in Four Programs. *Archives of General Psychiatry*. 54, 730-735.

Milosavcevic, V. 1975. Compulsory Treatment of Alcoholism. *Alkoholizam Beograd.*15(1- 2):112-115.

Minuchin, S. 1974. *Families and Family Therapy*. Cambridge, Massachusetts: Harvard University Press.

Nyhus, P. 1979. Right to Compulsory Treatment—A Possibility of Misuse. *Tidsski Edrusporsm.* 31(1):3-16.

Pepper, B. 1982. *The Impact of Uninstitutionalization on a CMHC: A Systems Perspective*. Paper presented at the annual meeting of National Community Mental Health Centers, New York, March 11.

Polick, M. J., P. J. Armor, and H. B. Braiker. 1980. *The Course of Alcoholism: Four Years After Treatment*. Santa Monica, California: Rand Corporation.

Read, Edward M. 1996. *Partners in Change: The 12 Step Referral Handbook for Probation, Parole, and Community Corrections*. Lanham, Maryland: American Correctional Association.

Reis, R. E. 1981. Effectiveness of Education and Treatment Programs for Drinking Drivers: A Decade of Evaluation. In L. Goldberg, ed. *Alcohol, Drugs and Traffic Safety*, Vol. III, pp. 1298-1328. Sacramento, California: State of California.

Reis, R. E. and L. A. Lewis. 1980. *First Interim Analysis of Multiple Offender Treatment Effectiveness*. County of Sacramento Health Department, Office of Alcoholism, Sacramento, California.

Reisman, F. and A. Gartner. 1977. *Self Help in the Human Services*. San Francisco: Jossey-Bass.

Rinella, V. J. 1976. Rehabilitation or Bust: The Impact of Criminal Justice System Referrals on the Treatment of Drug Addicts and Alcoholics in a Therapeutic Community. *American Journal of Drug and Alcohol Abuse*. 3(1)53-58.

Schofield, W. 1964. *Psychotherapy: The Purchase of Friendship*. Englewood Cliffs, New Jersey: Prentice-Hall.

Sheldon, J. L. and J. M. Ackerman. 1976. *Homework in Counseling and Psychotherapy*. Springfield, Illinois: Charles C. Thomas.

Van Putten, J. 1982. Dealing with Noncompliance in the Schizophrenic Outpatient. *Schizophrenic Outpatient*. 1(2):1-5.

Wallace, J. 1978. Behavioral Modification Methods as Adjuncts to Psychotherapy. In S. Zimberg, J. Wallace, and S. Blume, eds. *Practical Approaches to Alcoholism Psychotherapy*. New York: Plenum. pp. 99-116.

Ward, D. A. and K. J. Allivane. 1979. Effects of Legal Coercion on the Treatment of Alcohol Related Criminal Offenders. *Justice System Journal*. 5(1):107-11.

Zimberg, S., J. Wallace, and S. B. Blum, eds. 1978. *Practical Approaches to Alcoholism Psychotherapy*. New York: Plenum.

CHAPTER 5

Overcoming Offender Resistance

Glenn D. Walters, Ph.D.

Coordinator, Drug Abuse Program

Federal Correctional Institution-Schuylkill

Minersville, Pennsylvania

to Abandoning a Criminal Lifestyle

Incarcerated clients' tendency to glamorize the criminal lifestyle makes their unwilling-ness to change their thinking a significant problem for clinicians. Understanding the dis-torted thinking and perceptions of the offender client is essential for the therapist dealing with this recalcitrant population. The client's ability to self-delude is rooted in a variety of thinking patterns that are likely to be entrenched through repetition, occasional achieve-ment of criminal goals, and close association with other criminal thinkers. This chapter outlines thinking patterns that clinicians are most likely to encounter in offender clients, and it offers specific therapeutic interventions for each.

Offender populations are resistant and involuntary almost by definition. Whether we encounter such individuals in a correctional facility or community setting, most are, at best, ambivalent about change. Many arrive at the psychologist's or counselor's office with designs of securing special privileges, to include requests for a favorable parole recommendation in an institutional setting, or demands for a clean bill of mental health to satisfy a spouse or employer in a community setting. Whatever the motivation, the offender's presence in the counselor's office is the first step in the change process, a step that can be capitalized on if the professional helper knows how to deal effectively with the offender's propensity to resist change.

A primary cause of offender resistance to change is the highly reinforcing nature of crime. Instead of saving up the money to buy a car, the offender will rob a bank or store, pay for the car in cash, and avoid the hassle of securing a bank loan or making monthly payments. When one engages in a criminal lifestyle, there is no need to work out a problem or dispute; it is easier to belittle, verbally assault, or—in extreme cases—inflict physical damage on the nettlesome party. To combat the immediate gratification furnished by a criminal lifestyle, the counselor or helper must clarify the long-term destructive consequences of antisocial conduct for criminal justice clients and expose the lifestyle's erroneous roots (that is, criminal thinking).

It is important to understand that the criminal lifestyle is a caricature or ideal that criminals approach but never fully reproduce. No matter how committed a person may be to the goals of this lifestyle, he or she will fall short of realizing the lifestyle in its entirety. Some individuals, nevertheless, approximate this ideal. The closer a per-son comes to achieving the prototypic criminal lifestyle, the more the specific fea-tures of the lifestyle characterize the individual's actions. We stop short of labeling the person a lifestyle criminal, however, because labeling can become a self-fulfilling prophecy (with the power to inhibit change.) Lifestyle theory labels the lifestyle itself rather than the person (Walters, 1998). The criteria by which we might judge how close a person approximates the criminal lifestyle ideal is taken up in the next section.

Defining the Criminal Lifestyle

The criminal lifestyle is defined by four interactive characteristics: irresponsibility, self-indulgence, interpersonal intrusiveness, and social rule breaking (Walters, 1990). Irresponsibility entails a lack of accountability for one's actions and failure to meet certain personal obligations. Whereas many people are irresponsible some of the time, those persons with significant criminal lifestyle involvements, commitments, and identifications are irresponsible much of the time.

Self-indulgence represents a willingness on the part of the individual to sacrifice long-term success for the opportunity to achieve short-term gratification. Substance abuse, sexual promiscuity, and gambling are prime examples of the self-indulgence commonly observed in a criminal lifestyle.

Interpersonal intrusiveness is expressed as violations of other people's rights and is most clearly manifested in such crimes as murder, rape, and robbery. Some categories of property crime (for example, burglary or breaking and entering) also can be considered interpersonally intrusive. Individuals committed to a criminal lifestyle will deliberately encroach upon the personal space of others in order to pursue lifestyle goals.

Many offenders are known to have spent significant amounts of time circumventing the rules of the home and the laws of society—a pattern known as "social rule breaking." Whether the child steals money from a mother's purse, is suspended from school for skipping detention, or winds up in police custody for shoplifting, early social rule breaking can lead to an enduring and more serious pattern of law violation as the individual ages.

Conditions, Choice, and Cognition

Subdividing the correlates of criminality into conditions, choice, and cognition can be helpful in exploring the development of a criminal lifestyle. The conditions of one's life either can be internal (genetics, intelligence, temperament) or external (physical environment, family atmosphere, peer relationships) and serve to either increase or decrease a person's future risk of criminal involvement.

There is growing research evidence that certain factors, among them heredity (Walters, 1992), a difficult temperament (Olweus, 1980), and drug abuse (Harrison and Gfroerer, 1992), may increase a person's odds of becoming involved in serious criminality. By the same token, other conditions, such as above-average intelligence (White, Moffitt, and Silva, 1989), good parental bonding (Rankin and Wells, 1990), and positive peer relations (Feldman, Caplinger, and Wodarski, 1983) can protect an otherwise vulnerable youth from entering into a life of crime. Though conditions do not cause crime directly, they do appear to enhance or diminish a person's chances of embracing a criminal lifestyle.

If conditions do not determine criminality, then what does? Once we develop the ability to think and reason, even at a rudimentary level, choice determines our behavior, criminal or otherwise. Except when a severe mental or emotional disability limits our ability to comprehend the nature of our actions, we have the capacity for choice, although this ability evolves and expands with age and experience.

Under normal conditions, we would not hold a five-year-old child legally responsible for killing a playmate, but we would nearly always find a twenty-five-year-old culpable for such an act. This is because an adult is better able to appreciate the wrongfulness of his or her actions as a consequence of increased neurocognitive development and a growing base of environmental experience. Unlike the typical five-year-old, who is largely dependent on his or her immediate surroundings (nuclear family) for information about the world, adults have more contact with extra-familial sources of information through school, the neighborhood, and the media. Accordingly, adults generally enjoy a wider array of options than children.

Whereas conditions restrict our options, choice determines our selection of options. Ultimately, the selection process itself is influenced by factors external to the individual. However, it is a fundamental tenet of lifestyle theory that the human decision maker always has the option to avoid old reinforcement patterns and respond to new ones. If this were not true, behavioral continuity would be absolute, and change would be all but impossible.

To support his or her life choices, the individual constructs a cognitive system designed to justify, rationalize, and perpetuate the lifestyle upon which these choices are predicated. Developmental and experiential factors are of cardinal significance in understanding this cognitive system. The development of people who identify with a criminal lifestyle differs from that of their noncriminal peers in the sense that criminals actively avoid maturity, responsibility, and other early cornerstones of adult development. Experientially, people who engage in a criminal lifestyle are reinforced for criminal behavior because they see that it produces immediate results, although they often fail to take into account the negative long-term consequences of their actions because of their immaturity. The thinking that maintains a criminal lifestyle and supports resistance to change is defined by eight thinking styles: mollification, cutoff, entitlement, power orientation, sentimentality, superoptimism, cognitive indolence, and discontinuity (*see* Table 1 on page 82).

Resistance and the Criminal Lifestyle

Resistance is commonly defined as opposing, contesting, or withstanding the ideas, actions, or wishes of another. The high-rate offender has spent a lifetime opposing the ideas, actions, and wishes of others, and resisting change most of all. This is because altering thoughts and behaviors that have become the sustenance of one's lifestyle can be both frightening and extremely difficult.

Over the course of violating the laws of society and the personal rights of others, people committed to a criminal lifestyle have formed a protective shield of justifications, rationalizations, and excuses for their behaviors. Nullifying this resistance will require a maximum degree of patience and commitment on the part of the counselor or helper. This will entail dealing with resistance at the following three levels:

- Resistance based on the conditions of one's life
- Resistance based on the choices one has made and continues to make relative to these conditions
- Resistance based on the thinking styles that have evolved in support of the choices one has made relative to the criminal lifestyle

Condition-based Resistance

Conditions are factors that we must learn to accept (such as death), avoid (such as criminal opportunity), or change (such as drug use). Many

Table 1 —
Eight Thinking Styles that Support a Criminal Lifestyle

Thinking Style	Description	Suggested Strategies
Mollification	Rationalizing or justifying past criminal actions by pointing to societal injustices, the failings of others, or by blaming the victims of one's crimes.	Confront rationalizations with facts; provide feedback designed to strip away self-deception.
Cutoff (Implosion)	Rapid elimination of deterrents to criminal action. The cutoff can either be internal or external.	Coping skills training; teach client how to develop self-control and prevent build-up of emotion by dealing with issues as they arise.
Entitlement	Belief that one is entitled to violate the laws of society or the personal rights of others by virtue of ownership, personal uniqueness, or misidentification of wants as needs.	Challenge attitude of ownership and privilege; help client learn to differentiate between wants and needs.
Power Orientation	Attempts to gain a sense of power and control over the external environment; the absence of power being experienced as a zero state that the individual attempts to overcome by power thrusting.	Encourage self-discipline and the development of an internal locus of control; teach client alternative ways to handle zero state feelings.

Table 1 — (Con't)
Eight Thinking Styles that Support a Criminal Lifestyle

Thinking Style	Description	Suggested Strategies
Sentimentality	Pointing out the positive things one has done to justify remaining in the lifestyle and not changing; also known as the "Robin Hood Syndrome."	Teach client the difference between sentimentality and true caring and concern; encourage sacrifice and nonselfish ways of interacting with the environment.
Superoptimism	Belief that one can continue in a criminal lifestyle without experiencing the negative consequences of that lifestyle (e.g., arrest, imprisonment, death).	Confront the unrealistic beliefs and expectations that buttress superoptimism; provide client with regular feedback on the feasibility of his or her plans.
Cognitive Indolence	Lazy, noncritical thinking grounded in generalities; shortcuts are the preferred means to an end for someone operating on the basis of cognitive indolence.	Training in critical reasoning skills, means-ends thinking, cost-benefit analysis, and goal setting.
Discontinuity	Lack of consistency, congruence, or continuity in one's thinking, which leads one to become easily side-tracked and have trouble staying focused and following through on initial intentions; can give rise to a "Jekyll and Hyde" persona.	Self-monitoring of ongoing thoughts and provision of structured programming to help keep the client focused.

high-rate offenders sabotage their own best efforts to change by focusing their attention on external conditions and complaining that they never had a chance in life. The helper must be careful to avoid the trap of nonproductive discussions of a person's early life, for it tends to reinforce fatalism and self-pity. The jail or prison environment also lends itself to certain counter-change influences. Other criminals, many of whom encourage external attributions for the causes of their behavior, surround the offender. Walters and White (1988) discuss several ways in which the correctional environment might be modified for the purpose of teaching attributes and skills many offenders lack (such as responsibility, self-restraint, and interpersonal problem solving). However, we must refrain from protracted discussions on early life experiences because it can easily divert attention from the task at hand, which is helping offenders change their behavior by changing their thinking.

To limit condition-based resistance, the helper should listen attentively, be straightforward, and make it clear to the offender that change is possible. What sets the lifestyle approach to intervention apart from more traditional forms of psychotherapy is that it places a premium on the direct application of cognitive and behavioral principles, is largely didactic in nature, and appreciates the value of confrontation in promoting behavioral change. The emphasis of this system of assisted change is on the "here and now" rather than on the past. Helpers using this approach are encouraged to challenge sundry aspects of criminal thought without being overly critical or judgmental. Hence, where an offender might claim that he or she was a victim of nefarious personal and social conditions, the counselor or helper will want to point out that this statement is founded on assumptions the individual may want to examine more closely.

Choice-based Resistance

A major obstacle to change in incarcerated offenders is the belief that they had no choice but to engage in the criminal act for which they are currently facing charges or serving time. The alleged culprit could be poverty, peers, drugs, or an unfortunate home environment, but rarely do offenders blame themselves for what they have done. Some individuals will pay lip service to the notion that they were responsible for the consequences of their actions, although a careful review of their statements will often reveal rationalizations and excuses interwoven with assertions that they are responsible for their criminality. This is because those involved in a criminal lifestyle must deceive themselves before they can deceive anyone else. They have invested large amounts of time and energy in constructing a system of rationalization that does not simply disappear once they are arrested or incarcerated.

In confronting choice-based resistance, it is essential that the major choices the offender has made in life be reviewed. The individual can then be made to realize that events do not occur haphazardly. Although conditions influence behavior, they do not determine it. To understand how behavior is determined, we need to consider choice and decision making. Monahan (1973) cites research intimating that people who view themselves as responsible for their actions are among the more successful and contributing members of the community. Helping offenders understand how their lives have gone astray as a consequence of criminal thinking and poor decision making, as is recommended by Samenow (1984) and others, is critical if choice-based resistance is to be surmounted. Such an approach, properly conducted, can become a vital link in a client's search for future behavioral change. It is difficult, even for the most hardened criminals, to ignore the fact that they have little to show for their years of fast living.

The initial stages of intervention with choice-based resistance are probably best handled in individual sessions with a trained counselor or helper. However, once initial resistance has been overcome, the more subtle and entrenched features of choice-based resistance can best be managed in a helper-led group. Such groups provide the offender with a great wealth of new information gathered from interactions with other individuals who have been previously invested in a criminal lifestyle. It also allows for the creation of an external feedback mechanism (offenders challenging each other) with the prospect of internalization somewhere down the line. The implementation of this internalized feedback mechanism is the primary goal of the lifestyle approach to change.

Cognition-based Resistance

Since resistance is largely a cognitive phenomenon, it should come as no surprise that it can likely be most effectively managed at the cognitive or self-talk level. The resistance observed at this level has it origins in the irrationality of the criminal lifestyle as represented by the eight thinking styles listed and described in Table 1. This cognitive system arises as a means of buttressing offenders' criminal decisions, thereby allowing them to resist more rational thoughts that would threaten the lifestyle's survival (Walters and White, 1989). Techniques and procedures designed to confront the irrationality of cognition-based resistance are manifold and will be examined individually for each of the eight styles. Where possible, specific examples of cognition-based resistance, along with suggestions on how one might help someone abandon the criminal lifestyle, will be supplied.

Mollification

The excuses and justifications that support mollification are prime targets for early change efforts with respect to the criminal lifestyle. Offenders will often direct their resistance to concerns about unfairness or societal injustice, or they may express their mollification by blaming the victims of their crimes or by minimizing the seriousness of past criminal involvements. No matter what form it takes, mollification must be challenged. If mollification is left unchallenged, the offender will continue projecting blame onto the external environment rather than accepting responsibility for his or her actions and taking an honest look at himself or herself. What follows are a few examples of cognition-based resistance expressed through mollification.

Mollification-1: "What happened to me was not fair!"

Comment: Unfairness is in the eye of the beholder. What is unfair to one person may be more than fair to someone else. Moreover, inequity is something that has always existed and, unfortunately, probably always will. Consequently, demanding that life be fair is arrogant and unrealistic. This does not mean we must simply accept situations we consider unjust, though we need not spend an exorbitant amount of time ruminating about things over which we have no control.

Mollification-2: "The police (FBI, DEA) did not play by their own rules in arresting me!"

Comment: Simply stated, two wrongs don't make a right. This awareness, however, does little to deter many offenders from engaging in mollification. They may spend hours trying to justify their wrongful actions by pointing out that some of those charged with the responsibility of upholding the laws of society are either breaking the law themselves or engaging in unethical conduct. What the offenders need to realize is that what other people do has nothing to do with them and that they cannot legitimately use others' misconduct, perceived or real, to excuse their own violations of the law.

Mollification-3: "Everyone does it; I just happened to get caught."

Comment: Chances are everyone else is not doing whatever it is the offender is alleging everyone does. This speaks to the high-rate offenders' tendency to think in extremes and highlights their limited experience with the world in that they believe everyone thinks and acts as they do. If, by chance, others were to engage in illegal activities with the voracity and dedication of the high-rate offender, chances are they too would find themselves spending an inordinate amount of time in jail and prison.

Mollification-4: "The victim deserved what he (she) got!"

Comment: Rarely does a victim ask for what someone identified with a criminal lifestyle dishes out. Although some victims may not have been as vigilant as they might have been in guarding against the possibility of being victimized, this does not excuse, mitigate, or minimize the severity of the victimizer's predatory behavior. Such a statement is nothing more than a smokescreen offenders sometimes use to cloud both their own and others' vision.

Cutoff

Self-restraint and frustration tolerance are antithetical to the cutoff, which is immersed in impulsivity. Many offenders apply the cutoff to avoid assuming responsibility for their actions and never learn to deal with situations in a mature manner—they just "blow their top," and others characteristically give in to their demands. Whereas this approach may be effective in the short run, it creates problems for the habitual lawbreaker in the long run. The negative consequences of this thinking style includes prison, divorce, and retaliation by others. Demonstrating the long-term negative consequences of cutoff-mediated resistance should figure prominently in any program of effective assisted change.

In discussing the cutoff, it is important to distinguish between an internal cutoff and external cutoff. An internal cutoff is a word, phrase, image, or musical theme employed by the offender to eliminate common deterrents to criminal action. In confronting the internal cutoff, it is imperative that helpers teach clients to challenge their thinking by asking themselves the following two questions:

1. Is the cutoff based on a rational understanding of the current situation?
2. Will the action that ensues from the cutoff result in the achievement of both short- and long-range goals?

External cutoffs are exterior objects introduced by the criminal to deflate or eliminate deterrents to crime. Drugs and alcohol are by far the most common forms of external cutoffs. External cutoffs are best challenged by avoiding situations and objects (for example, drugs or pornography) that are known to fuel cutoff thinking in a variety of offenders.

Entitlement

Many offenders tell themselves that they are entitled to take things that do not belong to them, violate the laws of society, and intrude on the personal lives of others. They accomplish this by extending personal ownership to others' property, convincing themselves of their own uniqueness, or by misidentifying wants as needs. The following are several examples of entitlement-based resistance and how one might proceed with offenders who express such sentiments.

Entitlement-1: "But I'm different."

Comment: Some offenders reach the conclusion relatively early in life that they are unique, special people for whom the laws and dictates of society do not apply. However, as they find themselves continually in trouble with the law—including regular trips to jail and prison—reality gradually begins to set in. For this reason, it is not uncommon to see entitlement-based resistance, as reflected in protestations of one's uniqueness, decline with age. A principal goal of any program of assisted change is to bring this awareness to younger offenders who may have not come to this realization on their own.

Entitlement-2: "Society owes me!"

Comment: This sentiment is particularly strong among offenders finishing up multi-year sentences. Such individuals act as if it is society's fault that they have spent the last several years in prison. They contend that society "owes" them and that if they cannot get what they believe they are entitled to legally, they will take what they want. While there is nothing wrong with pursuing legitimate opportunities in the community, to achieve lasting success people previously committed to a criminal lifestyle must adopt the attitude that society owes them nothing. From this point, they can then begin the long process of building a new life for themselves.

Entitlement-3: "I need a new house (late-model car, expensive jewelry, drugs)."

Comment: Basic human needs include requirements for air, food, water, shelter, and in some cases, clothing; everything else is viewed to be a want or desire. However, people committed to a criminal lifestyle grant themselves permission to violate the laws of society and the personal dignity of others by elevating their wants for a variety of personal, material, and luxury items to the status of needs. This is a major component of cognition-based resistance, for as long as the offender believes that he or she needs certain material goods, he or she will continue to violate the law to obtain these goods. What the offender needs to understand is that these material goods constitute wants, not needs, and that he or she is not justified in pursuing the attainment of these goods at any cost.

Power Orientation

Environmental control is a predominant theme in the thinking of people who demonstrate involvement in, commitment to, and identification with a criminal lifestyle. When such individuals are not in control of their immediate environment, they characteristically experience what is known as a zero state (Yochelson and Samenow, 1976). Criminals who find themselves in the throes of a zero state view themselves as helpless, hopeless, and impotent. To free themselves of zero state feelings, lifestyle offenders will often engage in what Yochelson and Samenow (1976) refer to as a power thrust. The power thrust entails putting someone else down physically, emotionally, or psychologically in order to feel in control of the situation. What follows are several additional ways offenders use the power orientation to resist change and hints on how this particular thinking style can be more effectively managed.

Power-1: "People are either weak or strong."

Comment: Offenders frequently adopt the oversimplified perspective that people are either weak or strong, and because of their preoccupation with external control, they value physical virility over mental toughness. It is essential that the validity of this belief be challenged because offenders use this type of thinking to avoid new information and resist the prospect of change.

Power-2: "I'm a zero."

Comment: Persons affiliated with the criminal lifestyle are no more total losers than they are all-powerful winners. However, they must separate themselves from this dichotomous black-and-white thinking if they hope to successfully abandon the criminal lifestyle. To accomplish this goal, habitual offenders must eschew their exclusive reliance on an external interpretation of events, for only then will they be in a position to avoid zero-state feelings and the impulse to power thrust in situations over which they have little external control.

Power-3: "I'm right and you're wrong!"

Comment: A power-oriented individual may resist change by throwing up an angry facade designed to keep the counselor or helper at bay. The professional helper might want to redirect the conversation to the issues at hand, asking the offender, "If it is true that you are so knowledgeable about this subject, why is it that you have spent so much of your adult life confined in various jails and prisons?" It is critical that we afford offenders who engage in power thrusting the opportunity to reflect on themselves and their desire to be in control of their environment. Only then can the resistance posed by the drive to win at all costs be reduced to a level where the individual can benefit from a program of assisted change.

Sentimentality

The "good guy" image that many offenders attempt to create is another cognitive factor that stands in the way of future behavioral change. High-rate offenders reason that engaging in certain positive behaviors somehow exonerates their criminal pasts. As is the case with all forms of cognition-based resistance, if we do not directly confront the sentimentality, change will not occur. This is because many offenders rationalize that as long as they perform good deeds, they are okay, their behavior is okay, and there is no need for them to change. What follows are several examples of sentimentality-based resistance and possible ways of dealing with each.

Sentimentality-1: "I've never hurt anyone."

Comment: The problem with this statement is that people involved in a criminal lifestyle are probably relying on a self-serving and narrow definition of harm when they assert that they have never hurt anyone. Often, what the offender means is that he or she has never injured anyone physically. However, psychological and emotional harm can be just as damaging as physical harm. Entering a bank wielding weapons and shouting obscenities will probably create emotional turmoil for bank employees and patrons alike, causing nightmares, anxiety, and interpersonal difficulties that may last longer than the bank robber's prison sentence. In saying that he or she has never inflicted injury in the commission of a crime, the offender is discounting the psychological and emotional harm this behavior has caused friends, family, past victims, and even the offender himself or herself. People engaged in a criminal lifestyle must become cognizant of the damage their antisocial actions create for themselves and others and use this awareness to stimulate future behavioral change.

Sentimentality-2: "I'm a normal person with normal ideas, drives, and goals."

Comment: While it is true that most offenders are normal in the sense that they do not suffer from serious emotional difficulties and that they seek universal human goals that most people desire—namely, affiliation, control, and status (Walters, 1998)—their actions are far from normal. In fact, the destructive potential of their behavior is so great that society has seen fit to segregate them from the rest of the population. Unlike many of their victims, those who identify with a criminal lifestyle have a choice—they can live according to the rules of society and remain free in the community, or they can violate these rules and spend much of their life in jail and prison.

Sentimentality-3: "What's wrong with doing nice things for others?"

Comment: There is nothing wrong with doing nice things for others. There is, however, something very wrong with using one's record of "good deeds" to perpetuate a lifestyle that victimizes others for the sake of one's own self-gratification. A potential strategy for challenging this particular aspect of sentimentality is to have clients draw a line down the middle of a piece of paper. On the left side of the page, list all the positive things they have done as part of the lifestyle, and on the right side, all the negative consequences that have arisen as a result of their involvement in this lifestyle. Once this is accomplished, the helper can ask the client whether he or she believes that the items in the left-hand column absolve them of responsibility for events portrayed in the right-hand column of the paper. Assuming a reasonable degree of open-mindedness, what the client can learn from this exercise is that sentimental acts neither compensate for nor eliminate the negative consequences of a criminal lifestyle.

Superoptimism

The resistance provided by superoptimism is reflected in the fact that many offenders never seriously contemplate change based on the belief that they will be able to indefinitely avoid the negative long-term consequences of their criminal behavior. If because of irresponsibility and financial mismanagement people find themselves short of funds, robbing a store or burglarizing a home may seem the logical solution, with little concern for the prospect of arrest or apprehension. If they do get caught, they resist change by convincing themselves that they will be able to "beat the case." If convicted, they will deceive themselves further by using superoptimism to bank on a sentence reduction or early parole. What follows are two additional examples of how people committed to a criminal lifestyle use superoptimism to resist change.

Superoptimism-1: "No matter what, I'll get away."

Comment: An offender's superoptimistic attitude is based on past experience. Research indicates that offenders get away with the majority of their crimes (Walters, 1990). This is because the American system of jurisprudence is more concerned with protecting the innocent than prosecuting the guilty, although some might argue that the pendulum on this issue has shifted in recent years. Although people get away with many more crimes than they get caught for, the criminal actions of someone involved in a criminal lifestyle are so repetitive (sometimes to the point of victimizing the same person, house, or store) that they eventually get caught. Until high-rate offenders realize the self-destructive nature of their superoptimism, they will continue to resist change because they are operating on the mistaken belief that they can get away with just about any crime.

Superoptimism-2: In referring to jail or prison, the lifestyle criminal may retort, "This is nothing."

Comment: Like most expressions of superoptimism, this statement is partially true, although clearly distorted. Most recidivistic lawbreakers upon their initial encounter with jail or detention, often as a juvenile, report that the experience of jail was not as frightening or uncomfortable as they had first imagined. Consequently, most lose their fear of criminal sanctions at an early age. However, to infer that the prison experience is "nothing" is probably not true for many incarcerated offenders, particularly as they approach midlife. Typically, as offenders grow older, they no longer find prison life as exciting and stimulating as they once did. As a result, they begin to fear the prospect of dying in prison. The fear of dying in prison may actually hold the same deterrent value for offenders as fear of incarceration holds for many noncriminals.

Cognitive Indolence

Persons involved in a criminal lifestyle are often as lazy in thought as they are in action. This laziness of thought, referred to by lifestyle theory as *cognitive indolence*, sets the stage for relapse. Offenders exhibiting a moderately high degree of cognitive indolence fail to challenge their thinking effectively. This, in turn, allows other features of criminal thinking to take root. Before long, criminals with good initial intentions may find themselves in trouble with the law because they believed that they had their problems under control and so stopped challenging their thinking.

Indolence-1: "It's easier to avoid obligations than to meet them."

Comment: This illustrates the nearsightedness of criminal perception. While it may seem easier to drop out of school, quit a job, or avoid paying the phone bill, these short-term solutions to life situations eventually will probably result in long-term difficulties for anyone who follows these shortcuts. The individual will then take even more drastic steps in an attempt to solve the problems he or she has created. This might include picking up a gun, looting a store, or burglarizing a home. As with previous attempts at problem solving, such measures will create many more problems than they remedy.

Indolence-2: "It'll work out."

Comment: People who identify with the criminal lifestyle may tell their family and friends that everything will work itself out, even though they have no idea as to how they are going to pull this off. The goals espoused by the average high-rate offender are often lofty and unrealistic. In addition, such persons typically approach long-range goals with a short-range mentality and are easily frustrated when their efforts do not lead to immediate results. Many offenders therefore might benefit from instruction in problem solving and goalsetting. In the end, the client must learn to establish realistic short-, medium-, and long-range goals and then implement steps to attain each one.

Indolence-3: "Why take the conventional path when shortcuts are available?"

Comment: This statement speaks to the heart of cognitive indolence and demonstrates how resistant the individual is to adopting a conventional lifestyle. Many people who become involved in a criminal lifestyle prefer taking the shortcut as opposed to the conventional path, even when they know the shortcut is fraught with long-term difficulties. Cognitive indolence is simply one more way habitual lawbreakers set themselves up for failure.

Discontinuity

The discontinuity of offender thinking is probably the most insidious feature of the criminal lifestyle. Unlike mollification, sentimentality, and superoptimism—which reflect the content of specific thoughts—discontinuity is a process feature of criminal cognition. For this reason, discontinuity is troublesome to pinpoint and nearly impossible for the offender to identify. Like cognitive indolence, discontinuity interferes with effective problem solving and goal attainment. It also fosters continued involvement in serious criminality because it prevents the offender from seeing the larger picture and many of the actual consequences of his or her actions. The compartmentalization of experience that is central to discontinuity provides the individual with a portal through which he or she can resist attempts to bring about a long-range shift in behavior.

Discontinuity is not only the most difficult aspect of criminal thinking for offenders to identify, it is also the most difficult of the eight thinking styles to modify. Yochelson and Samenow (1976) recommend use of a moral inventory in which the offender jots down his or her thoughts and then discusses them with the counselor or helper. This would appear to be a particularly effective tool in the fight against discontinuity, since it provides the client with the opportunity to observe the inconsistent manner of his or her own criminal thinking. As is the case with all eight of the thinking styles discussed in this section, learning to handle discontinuity effectively is a lifelong process and one that requires continued attention if the individual is to remain free of legal entanglements.

The thinking styles, like the interactive styles described at the beginning of this chapter, can be ordered along a continuum and are believed to change over time and across situations. Therefore, while people may engage in these thinking styles to one degree or another, these styles are not endogenous personality traits but actually a complex function of ongoing person and situation interactions. Lifestyle theory is interactive in the sense that it explores the complex and self-altering nature of relationships that form between the person and his or her surroundings, rather than focusing on personal or situational factors in isolation. An instrument designed to assess these eight thinking styles, the Psychological Inventory of Criminal Thinking Styles (PICTS), has been introduced and has received preliminary empirical support (Walters, 1995, 2001).

Conclusion

Confronting resistance on the part of offenders committed to a criminal lifestyle is of paramount significance and requires a counselor who is willing to be both honest and direct. Honesty and directness are the hallmarks of an effective therapeutic relationship, irrespective of the setting in which counseling takes place. A two-way exchange is sought in which the helper solicits information from the client, shares personal perceptions with the client, and stresses the importance of the client taking responsibility for his or her actions. To make the most of limited therapeutic resources, assisted change programs should be time-limited and focus on providing criminal justice clients with the skills they will need to prevent themselves from relapsing back into old lifestyle-supporting patterns.

Perhaps the single most important element in managing resistance is the avoidance of extended debates with persons who demonstrate significant involvement in, commitment to, and identification with the criminal lifestyle. Helpers can point out the self-defeating nature of their client's actions and how continuing to engage in such patterns of behavior eventually will lead to imprisonment or recidivism. It is not the helper's job, however, to make the criminal justice client's decisions or to recommend which of several available options the client should select. Rather, the helper simply supplies the client with information, feedback, and understanding that the decision to continue in a criminal pattern or create a new way of life incompatible with the criminal lifestyle is the client's exclusive province.

REFERENCES

Feldman, R. A., T. E. Caplinger, and J. S. Wodarski. 1983. *The St. Louis Conundrum: The Effective Treatment of Antisocial Youths*. Englewood Cliffs, New Jersey: Prentice-Hall.

Harrison, L. and J. Gfroerer. 1992. The Intersection of Drug Use and Criminal Behavior: Results from the National Household Survey on Drug Abuse. *Crime and Delinquency*. 38:422-443.

Monahan, J. 1973. Abolish the Insanity Defense? —Not Yet. *Rutgers Law Review*. 26:719-740.

Olweus, D. 1980. Familial and Temperamental Determinants of Aggressive Behavior in Adolescent Boys: A Causal Analysis. *Developmental Psychology*. 16:644-660.

Rankin, J. H. and L. E. Wells. 1990. The Effect of Parental Attachment and Direct Control on Delinquency. *Journal of Research in Crime and Delinquency*. 27: 140-165.

Samenow, S. E. 1984. *Inside the Criminal Mind*. New York: Times Books.

Walters, G. D. 1990. *The Criminal Lifestyle: Patterns of Serious Criminal Conduct*. Newbury Park, California: Sage.

_____. 1992. A Meta-analysis of the Gene-Crime Relationship. *Criminology*. 30:595- 613.

_____. 1995. The Psychological Inventory of Criminal Thinking Styles: Part I. Reliability and Validity. *Criminal Justice and Behavior*. 22:307-325.

_____. 1998. *Changing Lives of Crime and Drugs: Intervening with Substance-abusing Offenders*. Chichester, England: Wiley.

_____. 2001. *Psychological Inventory of Criminal Thinking Styles (Version 4.0) Manual.* Allentown, Pennsylvania: Center for Lifestyle Studies.

Waters, G.D. and T. W. White. 1988. Society and Lifestyle Criminality. *Federal Probation*. 52:52-55.

_____. 1989. The Thinking Criminal: A Cognitive Model of Lifestyle Criminality. *Criminal Justice Research Bulletin*. 4(4).

White, J. L., T. E. Moffitt, and P. A. Silva. 1989. A Prospective Replication of the Protective Effect of IQ in Subjects at High Risk for Juvenile Delinquency. *Journal of Consulting and Clinical Psychology*. 57:719-724.

Yochelson, S. and S. E. Samenow. 1976. *The Criminal Personality: A Profile for Change.* New York: Aronson.

CHAPTER 6

Floyd F. Robison

Associate Professor, Department of
Counseling and Educational Psychology

Indiana University

Indianapolis, Indiana

Marlowe H. Smaby

Professor and Chairperson, Department of
Counseling and Educational Psychology

University of Nevada

Reno, Nevada

Gary L. Donovan

Director, Career Center

University of Minnesota

Morris, Minnesota

Reducing Elderly Persons' Reluctance

to Participate in Counseling through Planned Influence

As the population of elderly persons rapidly expands, more clinicians are in need of appropriate skills for positive therapeutic interactions with this unique client group. Therapists are likely to have a dearth of personal experience when compared to their elderly clients. This seeming lack of life experience on the part of the clinician is just one area that may engender client reluctance to an open therapeutic relationship. This chapter outlines several such "differences" that are likely to inhibit elderly clients' willingness to partake of mental health services, and it offers specific examples of appropriate therapeutic responses, as well as a detailed case history of a successful therapeutic relationship's development.

The elderly (defined in this article as persons age sixty-five years and older) are the most rapidly growing segment of the population of the United States. The eldest members of the "baby boom" cohort (persons born between 1946 and 1964) will become sixty-five years old in 2011 and as this cohort reaches retirement age, the elderly population will reach 70 million by 2030 (Sheikh, 1996). Thus, considerable attention has been given to developing models for providing mental health services to older persons, as well as counseling strategies and techniques designed to meet their needs as they adjust to physical, familial, emotional, and lifestyle changes (Knight, 1996).

Historically, many elderly persons have been reluctant to participate in professional counseling services (Ganikos, 1979; Ponzo, 1978). In this chapter, the term reluctant is used to describe older persons who do not seek or accept counseling services or, when they are in counseling, appear resistant or unmotivated to act upon their concerns (Ponzo, 1978; Waters, 1984). Community mental health services for elderly persons tend to be underutilized (Burns and Taube, 1990; Smyer and Qualls, 1999) despite evidence that older persons present significant social adjustment and mental health needs (Rabins, 1992). Reluctance to participate in mental health services probably is a contributing factor to this underutilization of services by older persons.

Why are older persons reluctant to use counseling services? Several reasons have been suggested, most of which pertain to differences between elderly and younger cohorts in terms of their exposure to the mental health fields, historical experiences, cognitive and emotional complexity, and attitudes about seeking help for personal problems.

Exposure to the Mental Health Fields

The general acceptance of mental health services as a resource for dealing with personal problems is a relatively recent social phenomenon. Current elderly persons have lived much of their lives during the early and middle years of the twentieth century, when mental health services were neither widely available to the general public nor widely accepted as a means for resolving "ordinary" concerns (Knight, 1996). Psychotherapy, as it was practiced for much of this century, was a lengthy, expensive, and rather mysterious process commonly believed to be for the wealthy "worried well" or, more ominously, persons with serious mental disturbances. Persons identified as having mental disorders were often isolated from family and friends, sent to mental institutions, terminated from their jobs, or otherwise stigmatized in their communities (Herr and Weakland, 1979; Lawton, 1978).

Many of the older clients with whom we work in our respective practices do not have a clear grasp of the purposes of counseling or the distinctions between a psychiatrist and other mental health specialists, such as counselors and social workers. Nearly all of these clients have stories and, sometimes, firsthand observations of family members and acquaintances who "had to see a psychiatrist" or were "sent away" to institutions because they had "nervous breakdowns," "went crazy" and the like. Despite the destigmatization of mental health in recent years, many elderly persons continue to fear that contact with a mental health professional is tantamount to making a public statement that they are not right mentally and incapable of managing their affairs.

Historical Differences

The elderly have lived through as many as four wars, a major economic depression, and rapid social and economic changes as our nation has progressed from an industrial to a technical/information society. In his book, *The Greatest Generation* (Brokaw, 1998), Tom Brokaw noted that the "World War II generations" are distinguished by their values of duty, honor, courage and, particularly, responsibility to oneself. Among many elderly persons, responsibility to oneself includes the belief that one should deal independently with one's problems and overcome personal obstacles through hard work and persistent effort. When help is needed, elderly persons may tend to look to sources that historically have been closely connected to their daily lives, particularly family members and the church. The notion of working on one's difficulties with a counselor, who is neither a family member nor pastor, initially may be antithetical to their constructs of personal responsibility and personal privacy, and an admission of weakness.

Also, most elderly persons have acquired a wealth of family and occupational and social experiences during their lifetimes. Quite simply, they have more "experience in living" than most counselors, who typically are in their young or middle adult years (Sheikh, 1996). They may resist disclosing their concerns to a younger counselor if they do not believe the counselor has the breadth and similarity of experiences to understand them (Blake and Bichekas, 1981; Waters, 1984). Thus, younger counselors must find ways to establish their credibility and expertise with elderly clients—despite clear differences in amounts and varieties of life experience (Knight, 1993, 1996; Smyer and Qualls, 1999).

Cognitive and Emotional Differences

As persons age, they tend to exhibit a shift in their perspective on time, from a focus on time they have lived to amount of time left to live (Knight and Qualls, 1995; Smyer and Qualls, 1999). This shift in temporal perspective is adaptive in that it enables one to assess the significance of a problem. That is, whereas a younger person may evaluate a personal setback as a crisis, an older person may evaluate a similar setback as relatively insignificant in the context of a lifetime (such as, "in five years, this will not really have mattered").

However, this same shift to focusing on time left to live may hinder some elderly persons' amenability to seeking help for problems that affect their current quality of life. For example, some elderly persons may not evaluate a problem as sufficiently significant to warrant professional help or resist dealing with problems because they are "too old" (Colangelo and Pulvino, 1980; Ponzo, 1978; Riker, 1981). A client recently treated for major depressive disorder by one of the authors summed up these attitudes quite well with the following statement, "When I was raising four kids, feeling blue and tired all the time would have been awful, I could never have made it. Now, though, it doesn't really matter. I can sleep all day if I want to, there's nothing I have to do. Anyway, at my age, well, I'm too old to change, I won't be around that much longer anyway."

Thus, we propose that counselors have four major tasks when influencing elderly persons to participate in counseling. First, they should acknowledge clients' wariness of the mental health field and reduce their concerns through early interventions that reduce the perceived threat of stigmatization. Second, counselors should establish their credibility and expertise as helpers while building trust with elderly clients. Third, counselors should work within elderly clients' time perspective to help them assess not only the significance of current problems but also to identify the benefits of addressing them despite having limited time left to live. Finally, counselors should acknowledge elderly clients' life experiences and create collaborative relationships through which they draw upon those experiences to deal with current concerns.

To accomplish these tasks, we have proposed that elderly clients must evaluate their counselors as credible helpers, that is, high in perceived trustworthiness, attractiveness, and expertise. Counselors can promote these attributes to elderly clients and, thus, reduce resistance to participating in counseling, through the planned use of their professional power and influence. In this chapter, we will describe several interventions to promote trustworthiness, attractiveness, and expertness within the framework of the Power Strategies Model (Smaby, Peterson, Tennyson, and Tamminen, 1988). The model describes influencing strategies that may be used in three types of professional relationships. After briefly reviewing the literature on power and influence in counseling relationships, we will describe the model, its implications for influencing reluctant elderly persons, and ethical considerations regarding the use of power and influence when counseling older persons.

Power and Influence in Counseling Relationships

Several writers have offered definitions of the term power in professional relationships and a consistent theme in these definitions is the ability of one party in a relationship to influence another. Although power and influence are important attributes of all relationships, we will focus throughout this chapter on these attributes as they apply to dyadic (for example, counselor-client) relationships.

Nyburg (1981) defined power as the production of planned influence, whereas McClelland and Burnham (1979) asserted that power is the desire to be strong, impactful, and influential in relationships with others. More recently, Smaby et al. (1988) defined power as the capacity to influence persons and/or events in ways that alter the patterns of relationships between individuals. This definition places power in an interactional perspective, in that one party's power to influence another is affected directly by the other party's power.

Atkinson and Wampole (1982) identified three elements of power and influence in counseling relationships. These elements are attractiveness, expertness, and trustworthiness. They defined attractiveness as a client's perception of a counselor as approachable and friendly. Expertness was defined as a client's perception of a counselor as having specialized skills and knowledge, and trustworthiness was defined as a perception of a counselor's perceived openness, dependability, and sincerity. Atkinson and Wampole suggested that a counselor's ability to influence a client is related to the extent that a client evaluates the counselor as having these characteristics. Given the association between power and these relationship elements, Smaby et al. (1988) developed the Power Strategies Model to assist counselors in selecting strategies to influence others (clients) in professional relationships according to the levels of attractiveness, expertness, and trustworthiness in those relationships.

The Power Strategies Model

The Power Strategies Model (Smaby, et al., 1988) describes influencing strategies in four types of professional relationships: indirect, referent, expert, and reciprocal. These four relationships are distinguished according to the levels of perceived expertness, attractiveness, and trustworthiness between the parties in the relationship. In three of these relationships (referent, expert, reciprocal), there are strong, moderate, or limited amounts of perceived expertness, attractiveness, and trustworthiness between the parties. Smaby and his colleagues suggest that counselors can use direct influencing strategies in these relationships. The fourth type of relationship (indirect) involves the use of indirect influence based on the absence of perceived expertness, attractiveness, and trustworthiness. Smaby et al. (1988) cautioned against the use of indirect influencing strategies in counseling relationships because these strategies raised significant ethical concerns about misleading and coercing clients to respond in particular ways. Thus, it will not be described further in this chapter (for a discussion of indirect influence in professional relationships, *see* Smaby et al., 1988).

Reciprocal Relationships

Reciprocal relationships are based on mutual exchanges between a counselor and another person (for example, a client). In this type of relationship, the two parties evaluate one another as having little expertness, attractiveness, and trustworthiness. Thus, actions taken in the relationship are not based on perceptions of mutuality, identification, reliability, or similarity. Rather, each party feels motivated to give in return for what has been received from the other. The relationship operates through each party's power to provide an immediate service, or meet an immediate need of the other. Likewise, each party is motivated to respond to the other by a desire for the other to meet immediate needs. In reciprocal counseling relationships, the counselor's power is derived from the ability to meet the client's immediate perceived needs when the relationship is established. In return, the client is motivated to meet the counselor's immediate need for cooperation and willingness to pursue the relationship further.

Expert Relationships

In expert relationships, the parties in a professional relationship evaluate one another as having low-to-moderate levels of attractiveness and trustworthiness, and a relatively high level of expertise. Each party appreciates one another's skills, resources, and accomplishments. Each party is motivated to respond to the other out of respect for, and faith in, the other's skills and knowledge, rather than high levels of mutual liking or trust. In counseling relationships, the client respects and values the counselor's training, experience, accomplishments, and skills as a helper, and the counselor respects and values the client's experiences, cognitive and emotional resources, and capacity for change.

Referent Relationships

In a referent relationship, the parties evaluate one another as high in trust, attractiveness, and expertness. They respect one another on the basis of their perceptions of similar characteristics, aspirations, achievements, personal resources, and experiences. Also, referent relationships are characterized by high levels of identification, co-modeling, and mutual support between the parties. Tasks are pursued collaboratively, with the parties feeling comfortable with confronting each other more directly and negotiating more widely discrepant approaches to completing tasks without concern that they will lose one another's respect. In referent counseling relationships, then, counselors and clients are motivated to respond to one another by mutual respect, liking, and trust and by a desire to maintain the relationship.

The three power relationships are conceptualized as developmental hierarchy. Relationships typically begin at the reciprocal level. As the levels of mutually perceived attractiveness, expertness, and trust increase, relationships progress to expert and, ultimately, the referent types. As relationships become increasingly sophisticated, it would be expected that each party becomes more motivated to respond in ways desired by the other.

The remainder of this chapter describes interventions consistent with the Power Strategies Model that counselors can use to reduce elderly clients' reluctance to participate fully in the counseling process by increasing elderly clients' evaluations of them as attractive, expert, and trustworthy. Some of these interventions have been described previously in the literature while others are derived from our experiences as gerontological counselors and supervisors of counselors who work with older persons.

Implications for Gerontological Counseling

INFLUENCING STRATEGIES IN RECIPROCAL RELATIONSHIPS

Generally, we have found that when an elderly client appears reluctant to participate in mental health counseling, the relationship is at the reciprocal level. The client may be hesitant or unmotivated to talk with the counselor, and the counselor may, in turn, view the client as uncooperative, frustrating, and difficult. In reciprocal relationships, counselors may use several interventions to decrease elderly clients' reluctance to participate in counseling. These interventions are described below.

Self-disclosing to promote similarity. Several writers (Corey, 2000; Egan, 1997; Ivey and Glukstun,1984) have suggested that judicious use of self-disclosure by counselors can promote initial rapport with clients. We have found that counselors can use self-disclosure to promote a perception of themselves as similar to elderly clients. That, in turn, enhances clients' perception of counselors' attractiveness. Further, we have observed that the most effective types of early counselor disclosures emphasize similarities of experiences and backgrounds (for example, having children, living in a particular area of the country, and educational and occupational experiences). Disclosures of a more personal nature are best reserved for more advanced stages of relationship development, as intimate disclosures may be perceived as threatening (Blake and Bichekas, 1981).

Advocacy/advising on less threatening concerns. In our work with elderly persons, we have found that a client who initially is reluctant to discuss emotional or interpersonal concerns often is receptive to receiving help with more immediate, practical problems. Dealing with a client's immediate needs reduces reluctance in the following ways: (a) by demonstrating a sincere willingness to help the client, (b) by communicating that the client is attractive, (c) by exhibiting trustworthiness in being available to advise the client or following through with an offer to advocate for the client to others, (d) by providing help in a nonthreatening way, (e) by acknowledging the client's ability (such as expertise) to act positively on concerns, (f) by demonstrating trust in the client, and (g) by demonstrating expertise to the client in dealing with concerns. In turn, the client would be expected to perceive the counselor as increasingly attractive, trustworthy, and expert and to experience motivation to raise other problem areas for discussion.

Using reflective listening to build trust. Several writers (Blake and Bichekas, 1981; O'Brien, Johnson, and Miller, 1979; Waters and Weaver, 1981; Knight, 1995) have suggested that reflective listening is an important intervention skill for building an initial rapport with an elderly client. From the perspective of the Power Strategies Model, reflective listening also communicates the counselor's willingness to "move at the client's pace" in pursuing problem areas rather than immediately attempting to diagnose and rectify a "psychological problem." In addition, we have found that counselors who take time to listen and talk to elderly persons about themselves and their experiences tend to be perceived as personally interested in the client and, therefore, more attractive and trustworthy.

Minimizing direct confrontations. In reciprocal relationships, counselors should avoid strong, direct confrontations of elderly clients' ideas or resistance to change. Although confrontation is a highly effective therapeutic tool in relationships characterized by mutually perceived trust and attractiveness, we have found that confrontation tends to be viewed as an attack and a sign of insensitivity by elderly persons who have not yet attributed those characteristics to their counselors.

Communicating at the client's level of understanding. Many elderly clients feel threatened by clinicians' use of psychological jargon during counseling interactions (Herr and Weakland, 1979; Knight, 1996). We have found that although the use of a professional manner when interacting with older clients increases their perception of counselors' expertness, counselors can concurrently enhance clients' perception of them as similar by adjusting their interaction style (such as choice of words and phrases) to that of their clients. This process of adopting clients' communication styles has been described by systems-oriented family therapists as "accommodation" (Minuchin and Fishman, 1981).

In addition to the strategies above, we have found that several techniques described in the Power Strategies Model can be adapted by counselors to develop relationships with reluctant elderly persons from the reciprocal level to the expert level. These techniques include (a) maintaining a professional appearance, (b) describing to the older clients situations in which other elderly persons have been helped with similar concerns (taking care not to disclose identifying information about other clients), (c) making references available to clients from other professionals who are acquainted with the counselor's expertise and in whom the client perceives expertness, attractiveness, and trustworthiness, (d) demonstrating knowledge and skills through workshops and other educational programs in settings where current and prospective clients may observe the counselor's expertise (for example, presentations on mental health topics at senior citizen centers), (e) addressing older clients by their titles (for example, Mrs. Smith, Mr. Jones) unless permission is obtained to use the first name, (f) allowing clients to address the counselor by title rather than first name, even if the counselor would prefer being called by his or her first name, and (g) using tactful, polite communication.

INFLUENCING STRATEGIES IN EXPERT RELATIONSHIPS

When a counselor has developed greater levels of perceived trustworthiness and attractiveness with an older client, and a moderate level of expertness has been established, the counselor's influence is derived from the client's willingness to accept the expertise (Smaby et al., 1988). Strategies to increase motivation within expert relationships are described below.

Making mildly discrepant statements regarding change. According to Smaby et al. (1988), a mildly discrepant statement is a form of mild confrontation through which the counselor suggests ideas that are slightly different from the client's ideas. Mildly discrepant suggesting is similar to the technique of reframing (Haley, 1991). When proposing ideas that are only mildly discrepant from those of the client, the counselor acknowledges the client's ideas as valid while proposing new ideas that are not substantially different and thus are more likely to be accepted and acted upon (Herr and Weakland, 1979; Smaby et al., 1988).

Explaining psychological processes. Counselors in expert relationships with elderly clients can reduce reluctance to consider alternative problem-solving approaches by discussing their conceptualizations of client's concerns and explaining the reasons for their interventions. By explaining the conceptual bases for interventions, counselors can acknowledge clients' ability to understand their own concerns. In turn, clients are more likely to respect their counselors' understanding and insight and respond more positively to therapeutic suggestions. As described above, counselors' explanations of underlying problems should be only mildly discrepant from the client's explanations and should be communicated in language that clients can understand readily.

Identifying clients' resources/skills for change. Elderly clients may be reluctant to attempt change in their lives because they are not aware of their personal resources to cause desired changes or because they underestimate the value of their emotional, cognitive, material, and "life experience" resources (Lombana, 1976). We propose that in expert relationships, mental health counselors can influence elderly clients by suggesting ways that clients can draw upon their resources to act on their concerns. Likewise, counselors can help the client identify realistic limits on types of change that can be achieved and suggest ways the client can obtain needed resources. By identifying available and attainable resources and acknowledging that there may be limits to the amounts and kinds of change that clients can cause, counselors can communicate that they are sensitive to the realities of clients' situations and that their interventions take into account the types of resources clients have available.

Using peer models to instill hope. It is sometimes possible to work with a reluctant elderly client with the assistance of another person who is the same age as the client and who has dealt successfully with similar types of concerns (Waters and Epstein, 1980; Waters, Reiter, White, and Dates, 1979). The counselor can use the "age confederate" as a model for more effective ways of construing the problem, identifying available resources for change, and identifying potentially effective problem-solving strategies. Moreover, we have found that although a counselor may not yet have established a sufficiently cohesive relationship with an elderly client to directly confront maladaptive or hopeless thinking, the peer is often in a position to confront, because of similarity to the client in age and experiences. Group counseling is another effective means of linking clients with their peers. Group work affords opportunities for elderly clients to learn directly and vicariously from peers' experiences, and experience curative forces such as universality of concerns and hopefulness (Corey and Corey, 1996).

INFLUENCING STRATEGIES IN REFERENT RELATIONSHIPS

Smaby et al. (1988) asserted that parties in referent relationships perceive each other as highly attractive and trustworthy. They suggested that, in such an environment, the parties expect each other to communicate ideas honestly and directly and are able to plan change collaboratively. Indeed, collaboration has been identified as an important element of effective counseling and therapy relationships with elderly persons (Knight, 1993; Smyer and Qualls, 1999). Accordingly, we believe that mental health counselors in referent relationships can maintain elderly clients' motivation to cause change by using the following interventions.

Challenging and participating. In referent relationships, we have found that counselors can maintain elderly clients' motivations by directly challenging them to act upon their concerns and offering ideas for change that are more widely discrepant from their ideas. By challenging clients to generate change strategies and act on them, counselors communicate confidence in the relationships and reaffirm sincere respect and caring for their clients.

Increasing counselor transparency. Earlier, we suggested that by disclosing selected information about personal characteristics, past experiences, and present life situations, mental health counselors can emphasize their similarities to elderly clients. In referent relationships, we often have found it useful and desirable to judiciously disclose more personally significant information about ourselves to elderly clients. Such information may include (a) our own feelings and thoughts about interpersonal situations in our lives, (b) personal concerns and ways we are attempting to resolve them, and (c) immediate feelings and thoughts about our relationships with clients. Blake and Bichekas (1981) have suggested that these types of counselor disclosures can benefit elderly clients in several ways: (a) by describing problem-solving behaviors that clients may adapt to their situation and use to generate further problem-solving alternatives, (b) by reaffirming trust in clients, (c) by helping clients realize that they are not unusual in having their concerns, and (d) by communicating genuineness to clients. However, counselors must ensure that their disclosures are intended to enhance clients' progress toward therapeutic goals rather than to achieve dramatic effect or to meet the counselor's emotional needs (Corey, 2000; Ivey and Glukstun, 1984).

Brainstorming. In referent relationships, counselors and clients are able to freely generate and test problem-solving ideas that are part of the counseling plan. Both collaborate in considering ways that traditional techniques (for example behavior modification, assertiveness techniques, ways to mobilize resources) may be modified or applied to best meet the client's needs and brainstorm creative solutions to problems. Brainstorming acknowledges the mutual confidence that counselor and client have gained in one another.

Involving clients as helpers to others. We have observed that as elderly persons successfully progress toward their change goals, they often become interested in helping others. Being helpful to others enhances elderly persons' self-esteem and sense of personal power, as has been found in evaluations of peer counseling projects

(Bratter and Tuvman, 1980; McCaslin, 1983; Waters et al., 1979) and "telephone visitor" programs (Robison and Robison, 1989). We therefore suggest that mental health counselors in referent relationships with elderly clients encourage their clients to enter into helping relationships with others, particularly relationships through which the client and counselor can collaborate as helpers (for example through co-counseling or with the counselor as consultant to the client helper).

Case Example

Mr. Ashe, age seventy-four, was a resident on the intermediate care wing of a nursing home at which one of the authors was a consultant/counselor. He had entered the facility to complete his recovery from a mild stroke and had resided there for approximately two months. According to the nursing staff and his spouse of fifty-five years, Mr. Ashe was recovering well from the stroke and his prognosis for sufficient recovery to return to independent living was good. However, during the preceding three weeks, he had complained of ongoing, severe abdominal pain and stated that he believed his stomach was "being eaten away by cancer."

He was intensely anxious and fearful that he was dying, and called for a nurse as many as five times each hour, demanding pain relief, or another physical examination by his physician. At his insistence, his wife stayed in his room with him most of each day from the time he awoke in the morning until he fell asleep at night. He refused to participate in activities and took meals in his room. His physician had ordered numerous medical tests, all of which revealed no physical sources of his pain.

At the physician's request, two professional counselors in the community had contacted Mr. Ashe and attempted to initiate counseling to treat the anxiety and explore with him other concerns that might be sources of his abdominal discomfort. Mr. Ashe "threw out" the first counselor from his room during the initial interview. The second counselor did not fare much better, as Mr. Ashe accused him of being a "young pup" who had "talked down" to him, and refused to meet with him again after the first interview. When this author was contacted by the nursing home administrator to consult on his case, the administrator stated that, if he could not be assisted in dealing with his apparent psychosomatic symptoms, he would need to removed from the facility and, possibly, be placed in a psychiatric institution when he was no longer eligible for nursing home care.

After agreeing to take the case, the author first contacted the two counselors who had seen Mr. Ashe. Both reported that they found him to be "whiny," stubborn, and quite anxious. They stated that his somatic symptoms, combined with his belief that he had cancer, were suggestive of somatic delusions and that he probably was not treatable outside a psychiatric facility. One counselor acknowledged that he had probably "put Mr. Ashe off" by suggesting that his symptoms were not "real physical symptoms" and attempting to explain to him the relationship between anxiety and pain perception in rather abstract, "psychological" terms.

Initially, Mr. Ashe was quite hostile upon learning that the author was a counselor, as he expected the visitor to be a physician sent by his own doctor. The author first told Mr. Ashe, "your doctor told me that you've been having a lot of belly pain. He asked me to help him figure out why it's there and work out a treatment that will stop it for you. But I know that you've already had a lot of tests and they haven't been able to stop the pain yet (emphasis added). I know it's frustrating. It seems like doctors ought to be able to figure out why you're in so much pain. I believe you're really in a lot of pain and I surely think you must be getting tired of having no relief." This statement was conveyed to reflect Mr. Ashe's feelings of frustration and helplessness, and to communicate that the author believed he was not "simply imagining" his pain symptoms.

Mr. Ashe relaxed and told the author that he thought no one believed him and did not care if he lived or died. He recalled angrily that he had been seen by two "youngsters" (the two previous counselors) and that, in his words, "they treated me like a crazy man . . . they said it was all in my head. One pup was talking eighty dollar words. I didn't get what he was saying at all, must have got it out of his college book. I don't need kids like you talking to me about stress or whatever, I need help!"

The author again reflected Mr. Ashe's feelings of frustration and helplessness, and clarified his belief that he was not treated with respect, particularly when he did not understand the clinical terms they used to discuss his symptoms. The author then suggested that , in some cases, abdominal pain such as what Mr. Ashe was describing, could be treated in two ways. One way, through medication, was an option that his physician would continue to explore. The second way was through behavioral medicine, in which the author might work with him to control the pain himself until a suitable medical treatment could be found.

The author stressed that the use of behavioral medicine was not foolproof and would take some time to work, but that he believed Mr. Ashe had a very good mind and much experience in dealing with pain over his lifetime and, thus, would be able to use the techniques to obtain relief, if they worked together to develop techniques specifically for his pain symptoms. This explanation was given using words and phrases similar to those Mr. Ashe had been using when describing his complaints. Mr. Ashe expressed relief that the author did not think he was crazy and that he could eventually be helped with medication or other medical treatment. With the additional assurance that his physician would continue to work with him while the author treated him, he consented to "try that behavior medicine thing, whatever the hell it is."

The author then suggested that to develop the treatment plan properly, he would need some background information, stating, "you know, only a fool would try to help somebody he did not know." He learned that Mr. Ashe had been a carpenter and farmer throughout his life, and took great pride in having constructed several homes in the community during the past thirty years. The author mentioned that, before attending graduate school, he had been an electrician and, at the time, was building much of his own home himself. Mr. Ashe brightened at this and proceeded to discuss his personal history more freely. From this history, the author learned two significant items of information. First, Mr. Ashe disclosed that he had incurred a spinal injury in battle during World War II and had been intensely fearful that he would be left to die in the field. The memory of this injury and accompanying feelings of fear and helplessness recurred during two periods in his life when he was seriously ill and had emerged again after the stroke.

The second significant item was that he had not wanted to enter the nursing home and evaluated himself as "old and useless" since his stroke. This negative self-evaluation intensified when he entered the nursing home and contributed to his belief that the physicians on his case were not taking his pain seriously. The author reflected Mr. Ashe's feelings about these circumstances and assured him that he took them seriously. The author also assured Mr. Ashe that he would contact his physician to obtain information on his progress from the stroke and likelihood of full recovery, and provide this information to Mr. Ashe in "English" (in other words, in an understandable language).

At this point, an adequate reciprocal relationship had been established and the author began to apply techniques to move the relationship to an expert level. Again using "plain English," the author explained to him a procedure that combined systematic desensitization and guided imagery techniques that would help him control his perception of abdominal pain. Essentially, the rationale for this procedure was explained as "letting your mind make its own medicine to turn off the pain when you want it to."

Mr. Ashe was initially skeptical that this procedure would work, but he liked the idea of being able to control his pain without depending on help from doctors and nurses throughout the day. The author suggested that they begin to try the procedure. First, they developed an image of a "peaceful place" that he would find relaxing (this was a scene of a cabin in a local woods where he often had stayed while hunting on weekends). When he was able to visualize this scene, the author taught Mr. and Mrs. Ashe a standard progressive relaxation procedure, involving progressive steps during which tension was created and released in the major muscle groups, each step followed by deep breathing and visualization of a relaxing scene. The author then administered the procedure to Mr. and Mrs. Ashe together. At each step of the procedure, while the couple breathed deeply and visualized the scene, the author provided suggestions that reinforced Mr. Ashe's belief in his ability to manage his own pain. Following administration of the procedure, Mr. Ashe acknowledged that he did not feel the pain while he was relaxed, although he complained that it returned immediately upon completing the procedure. However, the author and Mrs. Ashe reinforced his success in reducing the pain for a short time and Mr. Ashe recalled that he had done something similar to the procedure to distract himself from the pain of his wound during the war.

The author suggested that, in fact, Mr. Ashe not only had not lost his mind, but was able to control his body and assist his recovery process using techniques he had learned during his life. Mr. Ashe began to acknowledge, albeit somewhat grudgingly, that he had personal resources that may help him feel better on his own. He agreed to continue to work with the author on mastering the procedure the following day.

During the five treatment sessions that followed their initial contact, Mr. and Mrs. Ashe and the author continued to practice the relaxation/guided imagery procedure. As his skill in using the procedure improved, Mr. Ashe became able to eliminate his abdominal pain during the procedure and for increasingly longer periods after he completed it. The author and Mrs. Ashe frequently reinforced his ability to control his pain by drawing on his mental resources. Following the third session, the author gently confronted Mr. Ashe, suggesting that the pain might not need to be treated with medication or other medical interventions, but could be controlled by "behavior medicine alone." Mr. Ashe accepted this suggestion and agreed to begin using the procedure on his own using an audiotape. Together with Mrs. Ashe, the author and

Mr. Ashe analyzed the times of the day and evening when his pain was at its most severe levels, and he decided independently when he would use the tape.

At this point in treatment, the relationship between the author and Mr. Ashe was progressing to a referent level. Mr. Ashe continued to improve his skill in managing his pain. He identified portions of the taped relaxation procedure that seemed more and less helpful to him and brainstormed with the author about changes in the procedure that would make it more effective. During the next two weeks, the author used these revisions to the procedure to record two more tapes for Mr. Ashe's use between sessions.

Also, the author found it possible to make suggestions about the sources of Mr. Ashe's pain that were more widely discrepant from his beliefs. By the sixth session, Mr. Ashe was able to accept the suggestion that his abdominal pain may not emanate from a tumor, but might be a product of his fears of becoming useless and helpless that had haunted him since his military service. These feelings became topics in his sessions and he was able to verbalize his fears and accept the author's challenge to put his knowledge and skills as a carpenter to use upon his discharge from the nursing home.

At the conclusion of the sixth and final treatment session, Mr. Ashe reported no abdominal pain, was eating in the nursing home's dining area with other residents, and participating in various social activities. He continued to use the pain management procedure for several weeks before and after his discharge from the nursing home. Following his discharge, he joined the local Habitat for Humanity as a supervisor and worked on several homes with this group until his death four years after completing treatment.

Summary and Conclusions

This chapter described several interventions to reduce reluctance in elderly clients based on the use of planned professional influence. At the outset of counseling, elderly persons may perceive counselors as low in credibility, expertness, and trustworthiness and yet respond positively to efforts to help them meet immediate needs that may be viewed as minimally "psychological" in nature. By using influencing interventions associated with reciprocal relationships, we suggest that counselors can increase clients' motivation to participate in counseling and enhance clients' perception of them as attractive, expert, and trustworthy. As the relationship progresses, counselors can further use their influence to develop expert and, eventually, referent relationships, with related increases in the quality of clients' participation. However, although we encourage the use of influence to obtain elderly clients' participation in counseling, we acknowledge that the effectiveness of influencing interventions may vary according to counselors' motivations for using them.

The use of interpersonal influence when counseling older persons may raise ethical issues concerning whether it is a selfish manipulation of clients (Kotter,1979). Such concerns may be particularly significant when counseling elderly persons who are vulnerable to the actions and influence of others. However, a number of writers (Corrigan, Dell, Lewis, and Schmidt, 1980; Goodyear and Robyak, 1981; Heppner and Dixon, 1981; Johnson and Matross, 1977; Strong, 1978) have argued that interpersonal influence is an integral and desirable component of the counseling process. These writers have stressed that for counselors to use their influence ethically, they must be aware of their motives for influencing clients and sensitive to the effects of their influence on clients' decisions. In this regard, the Power Strategies Model conceptualizes influence in counseling relationships as an interactive process, meaning that counselors who wish to be perceived as attractive, expert, and trustworthy must genuinely perceive these characteristics in their clients. Consequently, we assert that if counselors are to successfully use influence to obtain clients' cooperation, they must be sincere when communicating interest in the welfare of their clients.

Our evaluations of these interventions have been largely limited to informal data gathering from our clients, members of their families, and social agency and health care workers who have provided referrals. Since developing this approach, we have observed increases (ranging from 30 to 50 percent) in the proportion of clients age sixty-five years and older in our private practice and community agency caseloads. In addition, client reports of satisfaction with counseling services have been consistently favorable, and social agency and health care caseworkers have reported improvement in our older clients' levels of functioning upon termination of counseling.

In one study (Robison, 1993), the use of planned influence in training/support groups for elderly diabetic patients was associated with significant improvements in patients' ability to control peak blood sugar levels, compared to performance of a control group. We believe that the current outcome data, while limited, are encouraging and provide a basis for conducting more extensive evaluation research. In addition, it is our intent that the influencing strategies presented here will serve as a foundation for counselors to refine the various influencing interventions and integrate additional interventions within the model.

REFERENCES

Atkinson, D. and B. Wampole.1982. A Comparison of the Counselor Rating Forms and the Counselor Effectiveness Rating Scale. *Counselor Education and Supervision.* 22, 25-36.

Blake, R. H. and G. Bichekas. 1981. How Can I Build and Maintain a Helping Relationship with Older Persons? In J. E. Meyers, ed. *Counseling Older Persons. Vol. 2.* Basic Helping Skills for Service Providers. Alexandria, Virginia: American Association for Counseling and Development. pp. 59-105.

Bratter, B. and E. Tuvman. 1980. A Peer Counseling Program in Action. In S. Sargent, ed. *Nontraditional Counseling and Therapy with the Aged.* New York: Springer. pp.131-145.

Brokaw, T. 1998. *The Greatest Generation.* New York: Random House.

Burns, B. J. and C. A Taube. 1990. Mental Health Services in General Medical Care and Nursing Homes. In B. S. Fogel, A. Furino, and G. Gottlieb, eds. *Protecting Minds at Risk.* Washington, D.C.: American Psychiatric Association. pp 63-84.

Butler, R. N. and M. I. Lewis.1982. *Aging and Mental Health: Positive Psychosocial Approaches.* St. Louis, Missouri: Mosby.

Colangelo, N. and C. J. Pulvino. 1980. Some Basic Concerns in Counseling the Elderly. *Counseling and Values.* 24, 68-73.

Corey, G. 2000. *Theory and Practice of Group Counseling, 6th ed.* San Francisco: Wadsworth.

Corey, M. S. and G. Corey. 1996. *Group Counseling: Process and Practice, 5th ed.* San Francisco: Wadsworth.

Corrigan, J. D., D. M. Dell, K. N. Lewis, and L. D. Schmidt. 1980. Counseling as a Social Influence Process: A Review (Monograph). *Journal of Counseling Psychology.* 27, 395-441.

Egan, G. 1997. *The Skilled Helper: A Problem-management Approach to Helping, 6th ed.* Pacific Grove, California: Brook/Cole Publishing.

Ganikos, M. L. 1979. Introduction. In M. L. Ganikos, ed. *Counseling the Aged: A Training Syllabus for Educators.* Alexandria, Virginia: American Association for Counseling and Development. pp.vii-x.

Goodyear, R. K., and J. Robyak. 1981. Counseling as an Interpersonal Influence Process: Prospective for Counseling Practice. *Personnel and Guidance Journal.* 60, 654-657.

Haley, J. 1991. *Problem-solving Therapy, 2nd ed.* San Francisco: Jossey-Bass.

Heppner, P. and D. Dixon. 1981. A Review of Interpersonal Influence in Counseling. *Personnel and Guidance Journal.* 60, 542-550.

Herr, J. and J. Weakland. 1979. *Counseling Elders and Their Families.* New York: Springer.

Ivey, A. E. and N. Glukstun. 1984. *Basic Influencing Skills, 2nd ed.* North Amherst, Massachusetts: Microtest Publications.

Johnson, D. and R. Matross. 1977. Interpersonal Influence in Psychotherapy: A Social Psychological Review. In G. Gorman and A. Razin, eds. *Effective Psychotherapy: A Handbook of Research.* New York: Pergamon Press. pp. 395-432.

Johnson, R. and H. C. Riker. 1982. Goals and Roles of Gerontological Counselors. *American Mental Health Counselors Association Journal.* 4, 30-40.

Kastenbaum, R. 1968, August. *Perspectives on the Developmental Modification of Behavior in the Aged: A Developmental Field Perspective.* Paper presented at the 76th annual convention of the American Psychological Association, San Francisco.

Knight, B. 1993. Psychotherapy as Applied Gerontology: A Contextual, Cohort-based Maturity-specific Challenge Model. In M. A. Smyer, ed. *Mental Health and Aging.* New York: Springer. pp 125-134.

Knight, B. 1996. *Psychotherapy with Older Adults, 2nd. ed.* Thousand Oaks, California: Sage Publications.

Knight, B. and S. H. Qualls.1995. The Older Client in Developmental Context: Life Course and Family Systems Perspectives. *Clinical Psychologist.* 48:2, 11-17.

Kotter, J. 1979. Power, Dependence, and Effective Management. In *Harvard Business Review: On Human Relations.* New York: Harper and Row. pp. 359-374.

Lawton, M. P. 1978. Clinical Geropsychology: Problems and Prospects. In *Master Lectures on the Psychology of Aging.* Washington, D.C.: American Psychological Association.

Lombana, J. H. 1976. Counseling the Elderly: Remediation Plus Prevention. *Personnel and Guidance Journal.* 55, 143-144.

McCaslin, R. 1983. *The Older Person as a Mental Health Worker.* New York: Springer.

McClelland, P. J. and P. Burnham. 1979. Power Is the Great Motivator. In *Harvard Business Review: On Human Relations.* New York: Harper and Row. pp. 341-358.

Meyers, J. E. and L. C. Loesch. 1981. The Counseling Needs of Older Persons. *Humanistic Educator.* 20, 21-35.

Minuchin, S. 1974. *Families and Family Therapy.* Cambridge, Massachusetts: Harvard University Press.

Minuchin, S. and H. C. Fishman. 1981. *Family Therapy Techniques*. Cambridge, Massachusetts: Harvard University Press.

Nyburg, D. 1981. A Concept of Power in Education. *Teachers College Record.* 82, 535-551.

O'Brien, C., J. Johnson, and B. Miller. 1979. Counseling the Aging: Some Practical Considerations. *Personnel and Guidance Journal.* 57, 288-291.

Peters, G. 1971. Self-conceptions of the Aged, Identification, and Aging. *Gerontologist.* 11, 69- 73.

Ponzo, Z. 1978. Age Prejudice of "Act Your Age." *Personnel and Guidance Journal.* 57, 140- 144.

Rabins, P. V. 1992. Prevention of Mental Disorder in the Elderly: Current Perspectives and Future Prospects. *Journal of the American Geriatrics Society.* 40, 727-733.

Riker, H. C. 1981. Gerontological Counseling. In J. E. Meyers, P. Finnerty-Fried, and C. H. Graves, eds. *Counseling Older Persons: Vol. 1.* Guidelines for a Team Approach to Training. Alexandria, Virginia: American Association for Counseling and Development. pp. 3-9.

Robison, F. F. 1993. A Support/Training Group for Elderly Diabetics: Description and Evaluation. *Journal for Specialists in Group Work.* 18:3, 127-136.

Robison, E. A. and F. F. Robison. 1989. *Evaluation of a Telephone Visitor Project Utilizing Nursing Home Residents*. Unpublished manuscript.

Sheikh, J. I. 1996. Introduction. In J. I. Sheikh, ed. *Treating the Elderly*. San Francisco: Jossey-Bass. pp xiii-xxi.

Smaby, M. H., T. L. Peterson, W. Tennyson, and A. Tamminen. 1988. Power Is Not a Four Letter Word. *The School Counselor.* 36, 136-145.

Smyer, M. A. and S. H. Qualls. 1999. *Aging and Mental Health*. Malden, Massachusetts: Blackwell.

Strong, S. 1978. Counseling: An Interpersonal Influence Process. *Journal of Counseling Psychology.* 18, 106-110.

Waters, E. B. 1984. Building on What You Know: Individual and Group Counseling with Older People. *Counseling Psychologist.* 12, 52-64.

Waters, E. B. and L. M. Epstein. 1980. No Person Is an Island: The Importance of Support Systems in Working with Older People. *Counseling and Values.* 24, 184-194.

Waters, E. B., S. Reiter, B. White, and B. Dates. 1979. The Role of Paraprofessional Peer Counselors in Working with Older People. In M. L. Ganikos, ed. *Counseling the Aged*. Alexandria, Virginia: American Association for Counseling and Development. pp. 229-263.

Waters, E. B. and A. L. Weaver. 1981. Specialized Techniques to Help Older People. In J. E. Meyers, ed. *Counseling Older Persons: Vol. 2.* Basic Helping Skills for Service Providers. Alexandria, Virginia: American Association for Counseling and Development. pp. 107-132.

CHAPTER 7

Cognitive Intervention

Robert R. Smith, Ed.D.

Professor

Marshall University Graduate College

South Charleston, West Virginia

Victor S. Lombardo, Ed.D.

Professor

Marshall University Graduate College

South Charleston, West Virginia

Treatment for Dealing with Domestic Violence

Clinicians in community corrections, jails, and prisons frequently encounter the domestic abuser client. The decision to deal with a variety of stresses through the use of violence, and to direct this violence to the domestic partner, is a subset of the criminal thinking patterns outlined in Chapter 5. Cognitive restructuring is necessary to counter the abuser's otherwise intractable belief in the rightness of his actions. The client's extreme reluctance to see himself as a perpetrator, rather than the victim of a "misunderstanding," also must be countered by the therapist. This chapter gives the reader an understanding of the abuser's probable cognitions prior to his assaultive behaviors and suggests appropriate challenges to such cognitions, based on treatment techniques of proven effectiveness.

The professional literature reveals that domestic abuse, in all of its forms, has evolved as a major social problem in our nation (Gondolf, 1985). According to the National Crime Victimization Survey, women are ten times more likely than men to be victims of violence inflicted by their intimate partners (Zawitz, 1994). Straus (1991) estimates that more than six million women in the United States are beaten every year, adding that the true figure could be doubled. From a historical perspective, responses to male batterers have been either to ignore, conceal, and/or condone their behavior (Smith, 1988).

It is important to note that researchers (Dobash and Dobash, 1979) indicate that for hundreds of years in Western society, domestic assault was accepted as a "husband's right and even his obligation." However in 1872, Alabama and Massachusetts became the first states to pass legislation criminalizing this form of battery. By the early 1900s, legal and public approval of wife beating had declined in Western countries and all states in the United States had outlawed spousal abuse; however, it continued hidden from the public eye.

Hall (1985) and others conclude that battery remains the single major cause of injury to women in contemporary American society. Some research indicates that the simple act of arresting men for their first abuse offense is effective in reducing the reoccurrence of battering (Sherman and Berk, 1984), but more responses are needed. Waldo (1987) suggested that punishment for spouse abuse has the potential to trigger subsequent abuse, and concludes that abusive men are often confused, frightened, and guilt-ridden about the domestic violence they have perpetrated. They, as well as their partners, are in pain.

Abusive males are then trapped in a destructive pattern that has severe, negative consequences for their mental health and adjustment and for their loved ones. They need supportive counseling and rehabilitation to help them recognize and change their distorted and destructive thinking and behavior. Researchers clearly point out that male batterers and spousal abuse are not unique to a particular socioeconomic status, race, religion, identifiable mental illness, or personality disorder (Goldberg, 1997/1998; Straus, Gelles, and Steinmetz, 1980; West, 1985).

Characteristics of the Abusive Male

Roy suggests that although abusive men are not distinguished by a criminal arrest history, more than 80 percent of them witnessed or experienced abuse as children, suggesting that battering is transmitted from one generation to the next (1982). Waldo (1987) has summarized three broad categories of abusive male characteristics that are important in planning intervention. They include:

1. Acceptance of the problem, from denial of the problem and resistance to change.
2. Personal adjustment, from remaining isolated with a shameful problem.
3. Relationships with spouses, often becoming enraged when spouses do not anticipate and satisfy their needs.

Violence is often rewarding to abusive men. In addition to relieving tension, it generally results in a momentarily "pleasing" change in their partners' behaviors (Giles-Sims, 1983).

A Cognitive-behavioral Response

A review of intervention treatments for dealing with domestic violence indicates that cognitive-behavioral interventions are the most effective (Smith, 1988; Smith and Lombardo, 1996). In 1996, Rational Cognitive Therapy (RCT) was included in the American Correctional Association's *Correctional Issues: Creative Therapies and Programs in Corrections* as one of the most innovative therapies in dealing with violent individuals (including male batterers). Rational cognitive therapy was cofounded by Dr. Robert R. Smith and Dr. Victor S. Lombardo in 1974. It is currently widely practiced in a variety of settings. Rational cognitive therapy is an effective intervention for dealing with male abusers because it incorporates key elements of two major types of cognitive intervention programs:

- Cognitive development programs (including problem solving, moral reasoning, social skills, and so forth)
- Cognitive restructuring programs (including distorted thinking, changing attitudes, beliefs and habits of irrational thinking)

Irrational/distorted thinking, poor problem solving, limited social skills, and morally ambiguous reasoning generally leads to criminal behaviors; including domestic abuse. The male batterer who receives rational cognitive therapy is shown how irrational thinking produces "upsetting" emotions that can lead to destructive or injurious behavior. The rational cognitive therapy practitioner trains the male batterer to conduct a rational self-analysis whenever an upsetting event occurs. More specifically, the rational cognitive therapy practitioner uncovers the male batterers' past and present illogical thinking by:

1. Bringing the illogical thoughts forcibly to the client's attention or consciousness
2. Showing clients how they (not their spouses or life events) are causing and maintaining their disturbance and unhappiness
3. Demonstrating exactly what the illogical links are for the client
4. Teaching clients how to rethink, challenge, contradict, and reverbalize such links so that their internalized thoughts become more logical

The following brief examples help to illustrate how rational cognitive therapy is used in domestic violence interventions and how the rational self-analysis is integrated into the abuser's treatment.

Case Study I

SELF-BLAME

George, a reasonably good mechanic, forgets to change the oil in a customer's car. After the customer notices that she was not charged for an oil change, she complains to George's boss who in turn chews George out for forgetting. Afterwards, George tells himself the following things: it was awful for him to make a mistake, he has done something stupid, and he cannot stand himself. These thoughts naturally lead him to feel worthless or "no good" and he quickly becomes depressed. George then continues to make more little mistakes throughout the day. By the end of the day, the service station owner is ready to fire George and tells him so. George leaves for home completely demoralized and ready to take his difficult day out on his partner. How might he have prevented this situation?

THE RATIONAL SELF-ANALYSIS

Ask George to explain what happened, what he told himself about his mistakes, and what feelings or emotions and behaviors resulted, particularly at home with his spouse. At this point, we show George how his emotions, and the resulting behavior, came from his distorted thinking. We also discuss how he could have prevented getting upset about making mistakes. Finally, we show how he could have avoided taking his emotions out on his wife. George's rational self-analysis would look similar to the following:

George's Rational Self-analysis

1. Activating Event or Happening.
   My boss chewed me out for forgetting to change the oil in a customer's car.
2. Self-talk or Opinion.
   How awful it was that I made a mistake?
   How can I be so stupid?
   I can't stand myself; I'm an idiot.
3. Emotions and Actions.
   Depression and mistakes. (Might there have been other things going on here?)
4. Rational Challenges.
   Ask "why?" for each self-talk item, such as "Why is it awful, the end of the world, and so forth?" Then, reason each of them out like this:
   It was regrettable that I made a mistake, not the end of the world. I will do better next time.
   Human beings can make mistakes; we are not infallible. We do need to learn from our mistakes and not make a lot of them, however.
   I can really stand myself; I have been doing it all these years.
   Work on other challenges, if applicable.
5. New Ways of Feeling/Thinking.
   Discuss disappointment, or other more appropriate emotions. Think through a strategy that will prevent reoccurrence of these types of mistakes, like suggesting to the boss that he have a work order which will provide a readily accessible list of things to be done and which can be checked off as they are completed.

Reassess how taking his feelings out on his wife by yelling and slapping is inappropriate and criminal.

6. New Ways of Behaving.

Use the checklist and continue to improve mechanical skills and work habits. Discuss George's new feelings and new approach to solving the problems employing the systematic way that rational self-analysis allows for problem solving.

Case Study II

INTOLERANCE TO FRUSTRATION EXAMPLE: SOAPY JUICE

Abbreviated Description of Situation

Matt asked his wife Mary to bring him a glass of grapefruit juice while he sat comfortably reading the Sunday paper. As a joke, Mary brought him the juice in a glass that the dishwasher had crusted over with soap. He became furious and threw the juice and the glass at Mary. The glass hit her and she later required six stitches in the emergency room.

THE RATIONAL SELF-ANALYSIS

Ask Matt and individuals in Matt's intervention group to come up with Matt's A-Event, B-Self-Talk, C-Feelings and Actions, D-Challenges, and E-New Feelings/Thinking and Behavior as though the situation happened to them; a similar situation quite possibly may have.

DIRECTIONS

A. Event

(Write down what happened-no thoughts or feelings here) My wife brought me grapefruit juice in a soapy glass.

B. Self-Talk

(Write down what you said to yourself - the "awfuls", "shoulds", and "can't stands")

1. She should not have done that; it is not right.

2. I can't stand her.

COGNITIVE RESTRUCTURING TARGETS

3. Add other self-talk that the individual or individuals in intervention might think of here.

C. Feeling and Actions

(Write down how you felt and what you did.)

Disgust, anger, and throwing the glass at her.

Might there have been other things going on here? Discuss this with the individual or individuals and then list.

D. Challenges

(Ask yourself why you told yourself those things in your head to come up with a better answer. Once you have, write in your better answer here.)

1. Mary did what she did (as unfair as it may seem or be.) What you really mean is that you wish she had not, an emphasis on wish (rather than should) will help.

2. You really can stand her, but you were not happy that she did what she did.

COGNITIVE RESTRUCTURING

E. New Feelings

(Write in new feelings.)

Irritation or other more appropriate feelings.

New Thinking

(Write in new thinking, for example, "What can I do using my head?")

COGNITIVE and OTHER SKILLS

Think through a strategy that will help prevent your throwing things at people who do not do what you would like them to do. Ask, "How can I control my anger better?" Maybe deep-muscle relaxation, deep breathing, stress inoculation, and so forth, in conjunction with the rational self-analysis.

(Doing your new thinking)

New Behavior

Treat such events or happenings as the jokes that they were meant to be or minimize the event by getting up and getting a glass of juice yourself and practice saying to Mary that you did not appreciate the joke, but it is no big thing.

What else might you do?

Case Study III

BLAMING AND CONDEMNING OTHERS EXAMPLE: SHAVING CREAM DILEMMA

Abbreviated Description of Situation

Don's live-in girlfriend had a habit of taking his shaving cream to the guest bathroom to shave her legs and never bringing it back. Don had to tramp downstairs while drying off from his shower and bring it back to his bathroom to shave. When Sally would ask what was wrong because of all the early morning noise, he would consistently shout back at her (something like), "You make me so _ _ _ _ _ _ mad, you shit!"

How might have Don handled the shaving cream situation differently? Ask Don and the individuals in intervention to respond using the rational self-analysis format. Produce the outline of the rational self-analysis on a chalkboard, wipe board, or butcher paper.

THE RATIONAL SELF-ANALYSIS

Ask the individual or individuals to come up with Don's A - Event, B - Self-talk, C - Feelings/Thinking and Behavior as though they were Don. Note: Here, too, the individuals in the group will have had similar experiences.

<u>*DIRECTIONS*</u>

A. Event

(Write down what happened-no thoughts or feelings here)

My girlfriend borrowed my shaving cream and didn't return it to the right place.

B. Self-talk

(Write down what you said to yourself - the awfuls, shoulds, and can't stands)

1. "Anyone who borrows things of mine should return them when I want.

2. I am nothing to her; she should treat me with respect.

COGNITIVE RESTRUCTURING TARGETS

3. She makes me mad.

4. Add other self-talk that Don or individuals in intervention might think of here.

C. Feelings and Actions

(Write down how you felt and what you did)

Anger, and telling her she "makes me mad," and calling her "worthless."

(Ask yourself why you told yourself those things in your head to come up with a better answer. Once you have, write in your better answer here)

D. Challenges

1. It would be nice if all people returned things when I want, but it

doesn't have to happen because I want it to happen.

2. I am something to her; she tells me so. This doesn't mean that she disrespects me. She may think that since the shaving cream is in the same apartment that I will be able to use it when I need it.

3. She doesn't make me mad. I do that with the way I process this event.

4. Work on others, if applicable.

COGNITIVE RESTRUCTURING

E. New Feelings

(Write in new feelings)

Annoyed.

New Thinking

(Write in new thinking, for example, What can I do using my head?)

Ask her how I can remain calmer in these kind of situations.

COGNITIVE and OTHER SKILLS

New Behavior

(Doing your new thinking)

Buy another can of shaving cream.

Do deep breathing exercises.

Summary

The rational cognitive therapy approach, if practiced, helps individuals to overcome emotional upset. The key to successful application is practicing the systematic approach over and over, through the rational self-analysis. With work, it will be found that life can be more productive and effective without self-crippling, anger-provoking, internalized statements and the resulting inappropriate emotions and assault behaviors.

REFERENCES

American Correctional Association. 1996. *Correctional Issues: Creative Therapies and Programs in Corrections.* Lanham, Maryland: American Correctional Association.

Dobash, E. R. and R. Dobash. 1979. *Violence Against Wives.* New York: The Free Press.

Gelles, R. J. 1977. No Place to Go: The Social Dynamics of Marital Violence. In M. Roy, ed. *Battered Women: A Psycho-sociological Study of Domestic Violence.* New York: Van Nostrand Reinhold. pp. 94-97.

Giles-Sims, J. 1983. *Wife Battering: A Systems Theory Approach.* New York: Guilford Press.

Goldberg, S. B. 1997/1998. Nobody's Victim. In J. J. Sullivan and J. L. Victor, eds. *Annual Edition Criminal Justice.* Guilford, Connecticut: Dushkin/McGraw Hill. pp. 61-66.

Gondolf, E. W. 1985. *Men Who Batter: An Integrated Approach for Stopping Wife Abuse.* Holmes Beach, Florida: Learning Publications, Inc.

Hall, D. L. 1985. Wife Battering: Dynamics and Counselor Implications. *West Virginia Mental Health Counselor Journal.* 3, 1-9.

Roy, M. 1982. *The Abusive Partner.* New York: Van Nostrand Reinhold.

Sherman, L. W., and R. A. Berk. 1984. The Specific Deterrent Effects of Arrest for Domestic Assault. *American Sociological Review.* 49, 261-271.

Smith, R. R. 1988. *Rational Behavior Therapy for Male Batterers.* Bradenton, Florida: Human Service Institute/McGraw Hill.

Smith, R. R., and Lombardo, V. S. 1996. Rational Cognitive Therapy in Offender Intervention. In American Correctional Association, ed. *Creative Therapies and Programs in Corrections.* Lanham, Maryland: American Correctional Association. pp. 71-77.

Straus, M. A. 1991. Conceptualization and Measurement of Battering: Implications for Public Policy. In M. Steinman, ed. *Woman Battering: Policy Responses.* Cincinnati, Ohio: Anderson. pp. 19-47.

Straus, M. A., R. J. Gelles, and S. Steinmetz. 1980. *Behind Closed Doors: Violence in the American Family.* Garden City, New York: Anchor Books.

Waldo, M. 1987. Also Victims: Understanding and Treating Men Arrested for Spouse Abuse. *Journal of Counseling and Development.* 65, 385-388.

West, J. 1985. Subordination of Women: A Historical Review. *West Virginia Mental Health Counselor Journal.* 3, 27-32.

Zawitz, M. W. 1994. *Violence Between Intimates.* Washington, D.C.: Bureau of Justice Statistics.

CHAPTER 8

Developing a Therapeutic Alliance

Flynn O'Malley, Ph.D.

Director, Outpatient Services

Menninger Clinic

Topeka, Kansas

in the Hospital Treatment of Disturbed Adolescents

Reprinted with permission from the *Bulletin of the Menninger Clinic* Vol. 54, No. 1, pp. 13-24. Copyright 1990, The Menninger Foundation.

Current treatment of the adolescent population is influenced by the media bias of viewing such clients as our culture's preferred scapegoats. It would certainly be understandable for clinicians to begin to view their adolescent clients through this distorted lens, as well. In reality, the treatment of disturbed adolescents requires a collaborative approach, where the therapist is willing to empathize with the clients' needs for protection from humiliation, their reactions to the coercive nature of their hospitalization, and their normal adolescent responses. This chapter offers insights into the obstacles to therapeutic collaboration and outlines the benefits that the adolescent patients derive from optimum therapeutic collaboration.

The concept of the therapeutic alliance has been most widely examined as an aspect of psychoanalysis and psychotherapy (Frieswyk et al., 1986; Greenson, 1967; Horwitz, 1974; Luborsky, 1976). Although the role of the therapeutic alliance in hospital treatment has received little attention in the past, several contributions have attempted to clarify the concept (Colson and Coyne, 1978; Frieswyk, Colson, and Allen, 1984) and to examine its value as an outcome variable in the extended hospital treatment of adult patients (Allen, Deering, Buskirk, and Coyne, 1988; Allen, Tarnoff, and Coyne, 1985; Colson and Coyne, 1978). These investigators have noted that the quality of the therapeutic alliance is a predictor of outcome and is reflected in its appraisal by the members of a multidisciplinary treatment team. Earlier work on the therapeutic alliance focused on the individual relationship between patient and analyst/psychotherapist, although complicated relationship patterns have long been understood to also exist between the hospital patient and the treatment team (for example, Kemberg, 1976; Main, 1957; Stanton and Schwartz, 1954).

In addition, there is ample evidence that qualities of the hospital milieu affect the efficacy of the treatment (Gunderson, 1978). It should come as no surprise, then, that in the relationship between patient and treatment team, there is both a general affective/interpersonal ambience and a sense of the degree of the patient's ability and willingness to actively collaborate in hospital treatment.

An examination of the role of the therapeutic alliance in the hospital treatment of disturbed adolescents must take into account the enormous divergence in treatment philosophies, program elements, and administrative structures in various settings. Some programs (especially those that focus primarily or exclusively on group phenomena, as in the "therapeutic community") deemphasize the central role of particular staff members (for example, the unit director, psychiatrist, or psychotherapist), whereas other programs reflect an attending-physician model in which milieu staff members are primarily charged with containing the patient while the "doctor" does the "real" therapeutic work. Gunderson (1978) argued that outcome is related to three ties of the therapeutic milieu:

- distribution of responsibilities and decision-making power
- clarity in treatment programs, roles, and leadership
- a high level of staff-patient interaction

This view of a multidisciplinary team working in collaboration, as emphasized by Berlin, Critchley, and Rossman (1984), represents the point of departure for this paper in terms of treatment setting and philosophy.

It may seem curious that the concept of the therapeutic alliance occupies a relatively minor place in the common clinical parlance and literature regarding hospital treatment of disturbed adolescents. In two major works, Masterson (1972) and Rinsley (1980) referred to the therapeutic alliance only with respect to the relationship between the patient and the psychotherapist, not between the patient and the treatment team as a whole. These authors simply may restrict this concept to the sphere of psychotherapy, or they may believe that collaboration in hospital treatment takes place primarily between the patient and the psychotherapist. It is more likely, however, that adolescent patients in general, and hospitalized adolescents in particular, are most typically viewed (at least in the initial stages of treatment) as being less collaborative and more antagonistic toward treatment than their adult counterparts.

Masterson (1972) referred to the initial stage of treatment as the "testing phase" (pp. 109-110), while Rinsley (1980) described this stage as the "resistance phase" (p. 23), both emphasizing the adolescent's tendency to avoid therapeutic collaboration. Adolescent patients who require extended hospitalization or residential treatment often fight against efforts to contain and confront their behavioral dyscontrol, and they avoid exploration of their personal pain and dysfunction because of character pathology, dynamic conflicts, and limitations in ego development. However, in addition to these case-specific aspects, the apparent lack of collaboration may pertain to legal rights or developmental factors.

In light of all these factors, and because of the nature of adolescent development, this author suggests that disturbed adolescent patients seldom begin treatment with any semblance of a therapeutic alliance, and that some fail to develop an optimal alliance even by the end of treatment. Nevertheless, precursors to genuine collaboration can be observed, and attention to these precursors can foster productive involvement in treatment. Some patients are able to progress through early stages to attain a level of genuine collaboration. Thus, by becoming familiar with the obstacles to such collaboration, the precursors to collaboration, and the different levels of true collaboration, treaters can involve adolescent patients better in their own treatment.

Obstacles to Therapeutic Collaboration

In the vast majority of cases, the adolescent inpatient's admission has been empowered by parents or other adults rather than by the adolescent. Pseudomature adolescents may feel that they are losing what few freedoms they have attained. More overtly dependent adolescents feel the trauma of a forced separation from their parents. As Weiner (1970) pointed out, "The adolescent has neither the naivete of the child nor the options of the adult" (p. 354). Adolescent patients (despite some awareness of their need for hospitalization) quite poignantly experience a forced hospitalization as a validation of their internal sense of powerlessness.

In addition to resistances to treatment that are rooted in psychopathology, hospitalized adolescents have normal developmental resistances. Two classic papers focus on the developmental dilemma of the normal adolescent. Anna Freud (1958) described the adolescent turmoil inherent in the attempt to defend against infantile object ties. Blos (1967) portrayed adolescent individuation as a process of disengagement from internalized objects. Both authors emphasized the "regressive pull" toward passivity, dependency, and resurgence in libidinal attachment to parental objects, focusing on the various defensive maneuvers and developmental accomplishments that adolescents employ to combat this tendency. Although other contributions (Kaplan, 1980; Offer and Offer, 1975) have significantly modified these views, the intensity of the struggle against regression and its disorganizing and frightening effect as described by Blos and Freud is certainly characteristic of more vulnerable adolescents who require frequent hospitalization.

A primary task of adolescence is the development of a sense of growing autonomy and independence while maintaining connectedness to parental objects. This ability is severely compromised in disturbed adolescents due to deficits in ego development and self- and object-relations, problems in self-esteem maintenance, and intrapsychic and external conflicts. Hospitalization becomes necessary because of the behavioral dyscontrol associated with (1) the rebellious stance of the pseudoindependent adolescent who has forced an early disengagement, (2) the anxiety and despair of the more symbiotic adolescent who feels unable to broach any real separation, and (3) the panic of regressive experiences endured by the psychotically vulnerable adolescent. In any case, hospitalization initially increases the youngster's experience of self as passive, dependent, and powerless. These ego-alien aspects of self are then externalized as resulting from the hospitalization.

Thus, there are three distinct sources of resistance to forming an alliance with the treatment team:

- the adolescent's perception that hospitalization is coercive because it is empowered by adults
- the normal adolescent revulsion against passivity and dependence
- the psychopathology of the disturbed adolescent, which heightens the reaction to separation from parents and containment in the hospital

During hospitalization, the patient and the treatment team often experience treatment as being "done to" the patient rather than as a collaborative effort. Nevertheless, follow-up research indicates that many adolescents establish a strong sense of relatedness to the treatment team and respond positively to hospital treatment. In fact, treatment inevitably goes well when cooperation and collaboration are ultimately elicited from the adolescent patient. The author's experience as director of an inpatient psychiatric unit for extended treatment of disturbed adolescents indicates that the therapeutic alliance begins with rudimentary, and often quite disguised, aspects of cooperation. These "precursors" to genuine collaboration can be helped or impeded by the actions of the hospital treatment team.

Precursors to Collaboration

Frieswyk et al. (1984) defined the therapeutic alliance in terms of "the patient's collaborative activity" (p. 463). Extending the concept to hospital treatment, Allen et al. (1985) defined collaboration as "the extent to which the patient actively uses the treatment process as a resource for constructive change" (p. 188, italics added). Collaboration involves active participation in treatment and, for purposes of this paper, can be distinguished from its precursors by adding the following: Collaboration involves the patient's recognition of his or her own contribution to problem maintenance and problem resolution.

In his delineation of transference and alliance concepts, Adler (1985) argued that:

> The therapeutic alliance in its mature, stable form is . . . usually only present in a later stage of treatment, although precursors or unstable forms of it may be visible earlier. . . . A sequence occurs in the successful therapy of primitive patients: (1) The establishment of stable self-object transferences that sustain them, (2) the increasing capacity to appreciate the therapist as a real and separate person, and (3) the gradual ability to ally themselves with the therapist in the service of accomplishing work (pp. 115-116).

The initial expressions of precollaborative behavior by disturbed adolescents in the hospital similarly are based on positive self-object and dyadic transferences. These expressions often occur in relationship to the entire treatment team or unit, not just an individual treater. Many adolescents progress from rudimentary levels of collaboration to more truly collaborative engagement.

By definition, precursors to collaboration do not involve the patient's active participation for the purpose of change, or acknowledgment of a personal contribution to problems, but they do reflect beginning (and often unconscious) aspects of cooperation and engagement. The following collaborative moves are listed hierarchically, beginning with the most rudimentary, but they are not "stages" of precollaboration in the sense that they represent a clear progression from one to the next: (1) acceptance of containment, (2) formation of attachments, (3) communication of symptoms, (4) collaboration in conflict-free spheres, and (5) developmental achievement.

Acceptance of Containment

Some patients demonstrate the most tentative beginnings of cooperation with the treatment team by simply accepting the containment of the hospital setting. Although these patients overtly rail against the containment and the structure, their rebellion is not severe enough to create a permanent sense of alienation from the treatment team or to result in their removal from the hospital environment (as might be the case with an elopement or a damaging assault).

Brad, a sixteen-year-old, powerfully built, aggressive young man, was brought to the hospital in handcuffs by police officers. He vowed to kill his frightened parents and asserted that the hospital would be unable to contain him. The treatment team gained some leverage through the patient's probation officer, who clearly informed him that if he left the hospital, he would be arrested and returned to court to face the charges against him. The patient's anger continued sporadically throughout his hospitalization. At first he was threatening and intimidating, but he attacked no one and did not attempt to elope. His threats became less frequent in later stages of treatment. He initially stated that he would remain in the hospital no longer than two weeks. He later modified his position to two months, then six months, and so on.

Containment and structure work best when they are established without ambiguity or ambivalence. Patients such as Brad also need protection from humiliation when they fail to carry out their threats and instead allow containment to continue. Those staff members and other patients who may have felt threatened and intimidated may understandably wish to point out how the patient has "given in," but such a reaction only erodes the patient's self-esteem and impedes cooperation. A more productive response is to regard the patient's compliance as "good judgment."

For patients to establish a sense of relatedness and to develop trust in the effectiveness of hospitalization, they must become convinced that their developmental needs will be met by staff members, who will provide containment, structure, and acceptance of dependency without becoming invested in control for its own sake. Because most adolescent patients externalize their experiences of dependency and passivity, they are hypersensitive to indications that treaters are overly invested in "showing the patient who is in control" or in keeping the patient dependent. An attitude that conveys the treater's interest in the patient's ultimate autonomous functioning in the context of supportive relationships can minimize, or at least avoid contributing to, the patient's perception that "you're treating me like a baby."

Formation of Attachments

Adolescents require relationships outside the nuclear family constellation to fulfill their developmental needs. Normal adolescents begin to loosen their internal identifications from parental objects and to invest themselves in experiences with other adults and peers. Disturbed adolescents in hospital treatment relate to various members of the treatment team through transferences and projections on the one hand, and through developmental needs on the other. Even the most disturbed adolescent makes an effort to engage in normal developmental activity. This effort may include seeking admiration for accomplishments, asking for help with developmental tasks (for example, homework), debating social issues, competing in skill areas, and inquiring about staff members' interests or views. A disturbed adolescent's engagement in normal developmental activity with members of the treatment team signals the beginning of tentative collaboration.

Jay, a fourteen-year-old boy, was admitted to hospital treatment following a period of social withdrawal, stealing, and escalating hostility toward all authority figures in his life. He refused to actively participate in any aspect of his treatment planning, and he required repeated interventions because of his behavioral disruption and verbal abuse of staff members. He learned that one staff member shared his interest in motorcycles, and he began to taunt and tease that staff member about their differing opinions on the quality of various motorcycles. This behavior was seen as the beginning of engagement.

Some staff members might want Jay to stop talking about motorcycles and instead discuss his problems, but imposing such restrictions could impede treatment. This patient saw no reason to discuss his conflicts until he could be sure that his developmental needs would be respected. Thus, although team members should continue their efforts to discuss problems with recalcitrant patients, they also should demonstrate a willingness to discuss some shared interest that might serve as a building block for later collaboration.

Communication of Symptoms

Authorities have long recognized that psychiatric symptoms can serve multiple purposes (Fenichel, 1945). At least two are evident in the behavioral symptoms of adolescents: (1) to prevent or decrease anxiety, depression, or other dysphoric effects, and (2) to reenact traumatic situations or problematic adaptations to learn how to master them. The adolescent patient's ability to produce and reveal manageable symptom patterns to the treatment team can indicate the beginning of collaboration.

Karla, a sixteen-year-old young woman with a long history of troubled and self-victimizing relationships with men, vowed at the beginning of her treatment to have no boyfriends during her hospitalization. During the latter half of her hospital stay, she formed a romantic attachment to a male patient on the unit. The young man lacked the sadistic streak of some of her prior choices, and the couple began to engage in controversy with the unit staff, who disapproved of their involvement with each other. Although members of the treatment team were somewhat disconcerted by this situation, it gave them opportunities to explore with the patient the nature of her relationships with men, and it gave her a chance to practice new ways of relating.

Some of Karla's interest in a boyfriend may have served to diffuse her dysphoric anxiety and her feeling of being unwanted, but her ability to collaborate regarding a conflict-laden sphere of functioning obviously had increased. The presence or absence of observable symptoms, of course, cannot be viewed as a unidimensional measure of a collaborative beginning. Some patients have so little ego strength and control over symptom patterns that they cannot avoid revealing this behavior. Their dyscontrol pervades the clinical picture and interferes with collaborative work. It is the task of the treatment team to encourage such patients to limit symptomatic behavior. However, adolescent patients generally experience less alienation from the treatment team when their symptom patterns are viewed as opportunities for work rather than as disruptions in treatment.

Collaboration in Conflict-free Spheres

Some adolescents who resist direct, active collaboration in problematic areas nonetheless may begin to express a willingness to work with team members toward success and mastery in conflict-free spheres.

Nick, a sixteen-year-old young man with a history of seriously disturbed family relationships, transient episodes of rage, and paranoid thinking, could not accept any view of his hospitalization that defined him as needing help. He defended against his fear of psychosis and protected his fragile self-esteem by expressing disdain of his treatment and treaters. He was, however, interested in playing the guitar, and he could not ignore the obvious expertise of one child care worker and a few other patients. His feelings of competence and control were not threatened by allowing others to help him develop a sense of mastery in this area.

When exceptionally resistant and recalcitrant patients can begin to experience achievement in conflict-free areas of functioning, it gives them "good feelings" about their treaters that gradually can lead them to work on more conflict-laden aspects of their lives.

Developmental Achievement

The intense structure and support of hospital treatment can elicit adaptive responses from vulnerable patients whose functioning would collapse in a less supportive environment. In a well-designed and well-functioning hospital unit, the consequences of one's behavior are much easier to predict, and the constant attention of staff members and peers ameliorates the patient's experience of isolation and abandonment. This sense of security provides the patient with energy and confidence to engage in developmental activities that previously were too difficult.

During the initial stages of treatment, Rick disparaged his treaters and disdained treatment. He was negative and pessimistic about any future for himself. He had been removed from several schools for his obstructionistic and aggressive behavior. Although he continued to express negative opinions on the unit, he began to achieve scholastically, started attending public school, and began to work toward a vocation.

School was truly a conflict area for Rick. He did not "collaborate" in his treatment by acknowledging a problem and working on it, but he was able to achieve in that sphere because he accepted the support of his therapeutic environment.

Most of these examples represent what might be called precollaborative behavior. In fact, some patients never progress beyond these "precursor" stages, yet nonetheless benefit from their hospital experience. One might argue that the degree to which patients engage the healthy environment of the hospital unit will measurably improve their ego development and the quality of their object relations. It also will substantially reduce their alienation from self and others, increasing the likelihood that they will return to a more normal developmental track. Other patients, however, can engage in more active collaboration.

Collaboration

As distinct from its precursors, collaboration involves both the active use of treatment for constructive change and the recognition of one's own contribution to problems. The definition of collaboration comprises a continuum of possible activities and attitudes ranging from patients' acknowledgment that they can have an effect on their problems to a real exploration of self in collaboration with treaters. In the former scenario, patients work to alter an external situation. In the latter, patients work to achieve personal change by accepting some degree of responsibility for their situation.

Improvement of External Circumstances

Adolescent patients who have achieved some level of engagement with the treatment team and who have become invested in their treatment program can begin to recognize their own contribution to difficulties at school or in family relationships. Although they may initially blame teachers and parents for their dysfunction, they often can gradually acknowledge their own role.

Lisa, a sixteen-year-old young woman with long-standing feelings of resentment toward her father, could express her hostility toward him only through verbal explosions that left her feeling even more alienated and less competent because her father viewed her outbursts as "ridiculous." Through discussions with treatment team members, Lisa began to recognize that her style of communication with her father relegated her to an infantilized position. She then prepared herself for an encounter with her father in which she could calmly and firmly express her specific dissatisfactions with his treatment of her, yet not attack him so vehemently that he would be unable to reflect on her message.

This case illustrates a level of collaboration in which the patient recognizes her contribution to a problem and takes some responsibility for its resolution. This type of work does not, however, involve any recognition that one's problems are aspects of self that are carried into any environment and that therefore require self-examination.

Self-improvement

Self-esteem is even less stable in the disturbed adolescent than in the normal adolescent. Such patients therefore must build up a significant degree of trust before they can engage in collaborative self-appraisal.

Cal, a sixteen-year-old schizophrenic young man, was acutely aware of his history of traveling from one institution to another. As his relationships in the hospital unit began to feel supportive and nurturing, he began to express a wish to adjust to life outside institutions. He was able to reflect on his experiences of becoming disorganized whenever he was subjected to external stress. He recognized his vulnerabilities, the usefulness of medication, and the necessity for a gradual return to community-based activities.

The type of collaboration illustrated here usually reflects a sense of engagement with the treatment team in which the patient feels a deep level of acceptance and a sense of being valued regardless of personal limitations or liabilities.

Exploration of the Internal Self

Some adolescent inpatients who have progressed well during the initial stages of hospital treatment are able to collaboratively examine aspects of themselves at considerable depth and with extraordinary clarity.

Sid, a sixteen-year-old young man who was desperately striving for a sense of identity separate from his parents, responded to their visits by engaging in verbal battles over minor issues of control, for example, whether or not he wore an earning. In discussions with treatment team members, the patient readily acknowledged that he enjoyed inflaming his parents and felt powerful after such encounters; yet, he was also plagued by feelings of guilt, abandonment, and depression. At one point during the treatment, the patient's parents went on a vacation by themselves, resulting in an extended period between their visits to him. During this time, Sid began to reflect on how powerless and alone he felt, and he recognized the level of his attachment to his parents and how fearful he was of ultimately leaving home.

Such insightful revelations can sometimes have an apparently brief effect on patients; their attitudes may vacillate and they even may demean the insightful experience. At other times, such experiences can be the cornerstone for significant and sustained change.

The therapeutic alliance in psychoanalysis and intensive psychotherapy is a concept related to, but by no means identical with, the disturbed adolescent's collaborative activities in intensive hospital treatment. To say that such patients have established a "therapeutic alliance" belies the realities of adolescent development, the legal and social aspects of the disturbed adolescent's hospitalization, and the gradual and tenuous nature of such collaborative work. Nevertheless, there are levels of collaborative behavior that, if recognized and fostered by the treatment team, can facilitate the treatment of these patients.

Moreover, the course of hospital treatment never runs smoothly from one level of collaborative activity to another. Just as disturbed adolescents may periodically go forward into higher levels of functioning while still struggling with earlier developmental issues, so does their collaborative ability periodically spurt forward only to retreat and then to possibly move forward again. Despite the unpredictability of adolescents' collaborative ability, the treatment team may enhance its effectiveness by advancing its knowledge of conceptual landmarks for judging aspects of collaboration.

REFERENCES

Adler, G. 1985. *Borderline Psychopathology and its Treatment*. New York: Aronson.

Allen, J. G., C. D. Deering, J. R. Buskirk, and L. Coyne. 1988. Assessment of Therapeutic Alliances in the Psychiatric Hospital Milieu. *Psychiatry*. 51:291-299.

Allen, J. G., G. Tarnoff, and L. Coyne. 1985. Therapeutic Alliance and Long-term Hospital Treatment Outcome. *Comprehensive Psychiatry*. 26:187-194.

Berlin, I. N., D. L. Critchley, and P. G. Rossman. 1984. Current Concepts in Milieu Treatment of Seriously Disturbed Children and Adolescents. *Psychotherapy*. 21: 118-131.

Blos, P. 1967. The Second Individuation Process of Adolescence. *Psychoanalytic Study of the Child*. 22:162-186.

Colson, D. B. and L. Coyne. 1978. Variation in Staff Thinking on a Psychiatric Unit: Implications for Team Functioning. *Bulletin of the Menninger Clinic*. 42:414-422.

Fenichel, O. 1945. *The Psychoanalytic Theory of Neurosis*. New York: Norton.

Freud, A. 1958. Adolescence. *Psychoanalytic Study of the Child*. 13:255-278.

Frieswyk, S. H., J. G. Allen, D. B. Colson, L. Coyne, G. O. Gabbard, L. Horwitz, and G. Newsom. 1986. Therapeutic Alliance: Its Place as a Process and Outcome Variable in Dynamic Psychotherapy Research. *Journal of Consulting and Clinical Psychology*. 54:32-38.

Frieswyk, S. H., D. B. Colson, and J. G. Allen. 1984. Conceptualizing the Therapeutic Alliance from a Psychoanalytic Perspective. *Psychotherapy*. 21:460-464.

Greenson, R. R. 1967. *The Technique and Practice of Psychoanalysis*. New York: International Universities Press.

Gunderson, J. G. 1978. Defining the Therapeutic Processes in Psychiatric Milieus. *Psychiatry*. 41:327-335.

Horwitz, L. 1974. *Clinical Prediction in Psychotherapy*. New York: Aronson.

Kaplan, E. H. 1980. Adolescents, Age Fifteen to Eighteen: A Psychoanalytic Developmental View. In S. I. Greenspan and G. Pollock, eds. *The Course of Life: Psychoanalytic Contributions Toward Understanding Personality Development, Vol. II*. Latency, Adolescence, and Youth. Adelphi, Maryland: National Institute of Mental Health.

Kemberg, O. F. 1976. Toward an Integrative Theory of Hospital Treatment. In *Object-relations Theory and Clinical Psychoanalysis*. New York: Aronson. pp. 241-275.

Luborsky, L. 1976. Helping Alliances in Psychotherapy. In J. L. Claghorn, ed. *Successful Psychotherapy*. New York: Brunner/Mazel. pp. 92-116.

Main, T. F. 1957. The Ailment. *British Journal of Medical Psychology*. 30:129-145.

Masterson, J. F. 1972. *Treatment of the Borderline Adolescent: A Developmental Approach.* New York: Wiley.

Offer, D. and J. Offer. 1975. Three Developmental Routes through Normal Male Adolescence. *Adolescent Psychiatry.* 4:121-141.

Rinsley, D. B. 1980. *Treatment of the Severely Disturbed Adolescent.* New York: Aronson.

Stanton, A. H. and M. S. Schwartz. 1954. *The Mental Hospital: A Study of Institutional Participation in Psychiatric Wellness and Treatment.* New York: Basic Books.

Weiner, I. B. 1970. *Psychological Disturbance in Adolescence.* New York: Wiley.

CHAPTER

9

Managing Patient Resistance to

George A. Harris, Ph.D.

Psychologist in Private Practice

PsychLogic

Kansas City, Missouri

and Noncompliance with Psychoactive Prescriptions

Failure to take psychoactive medication as prescribed is a common obstacle to effective treatment. But clinicians often may not know whether to attribute poor outcome to the medication itself or the patient's noncompliance. The purpose of this article is to outline reasons patients resist taking medication and to suggest strategies for increasing compliance. This article suggests that helping patients become active participants in their own treatment will reduce resistance and increase compliance with recommended medications, dosages, and scheduling.

Psychoactive medication is increasingly recognized as an essential tool in the treatment of many psychiatric illnesses. Even when illnesses appear to have social causes, such as a grief-induced depression, medication may help patients to find enough relief to use psychotherapy more effectively. Many disorders have a strong biologic or physical component, and medication may be the primary treatment with supportive therapy as adjunctive treatment.

Medication, however, cannot be effective if the patient refuses to take it or refuses to comply with necessary instructions. Stimmel (1997) points out that medication for depression, for example, appears effective in up to 90 percent of cases in controlled studies but is effective in perhaps as few as 50 percent of cases in clinical practice because of ineffective dosing and use. The prescriber is largely dependent on the verbal feedback from the patient to report effects necessary to adjust the prescription, but patients may be reluctant to communicate this information if they feel negatively about the doctor, the medication itself, or even the very idea of using medication.

Reasons patients resist taking medication as prescribed range from the simple to the complex. The following list comprises reasons patients refuse to take medication or fail to comply with instructions. The list is not rank ordered in terms of importance but does attempt to identify practical and psychological factors reducing effective use of medication. Some suggestions for countering these problems are also offered.

1. *Cost of prescriptions:* Cost may be a factor in failure to take medication, especially among indigent and uninsured populations. It may also be inconvenient for some patients to get prescriptions filled because of transportation problems or location and hours of a pharmacy. These factors should be reviewed when writing prescriptions and less expensive alternatives considered, for example, generic rather than brand names. Also, insurance companies often refuse to

pay for prescriptions that are not on their approved formulary. Consequently, it is often necessary to be sure that a prescription is on the approved list. Patients might be given the name and address of pharmacies that will fill prescriptions by mail. However, clinicians should be knowledgeable about any services to which they refer patients.

2. *Form of medication and route of administration:* Many patients cannot swallow large tablets or may not have the dexterity necessary to divide scored tablets. Suppositories are unpleasant for many and will be avoided. Obviously, many patients do not like injections. Medications that must be refrigerated may be inconvenient for patients who do not have access to a refrigerator, especially during working hours. Again, the clinician should attempt to consider the patient's preferences when writing prescriptions.

3. *Fear of addiction:* Just as there are many patients who actively seek medication to misuse it, there are others who irrationally fear addiction. Clinicians should be able to differentiate between addiction and dependence (for example, when prescribing benzodiazepines) and should be able to explain how medication is withdrawn when the need for it has passed.

Such fear of addiction may be related to core belief systems, especially those involving dependency issues. Many people develop counterdependency behaviors in reaction to their fears of being vulnerable to harm while dependent on others and thus will avoid medication that is perceived as creating dependency. Some patients arbitrarily may alter their dosage or scheduling to regain some sense of being in control of their lives without carefully considering or understanding the implications of these changes.

Psychotherapy may be necessary to uncover underlying issues such as fear of dependency that impede prudent use of psychoactive medication. Simple reassurance and explanation of the nature of medication may suffice in many cases. Clinicians may want to acknowledge to the patients how powerless they are to make the patient take medication on time and as prescribed to emphasize how much, in fact, the patient controls in the treatment process. Such acknowledgments emphasize the collaborative process that must exist in most psychiatric treatment.

4. *Fear of losing self:* As people fear dependency, they also are afraid that medication will take them over, cause them to lose their "self" and become another person. Such loss of identity fears manifest when therapists recommend other

psychological procedures, such as hypnosis, and are related to core psychological beliefs of anticipation of being overwhelmed and controlled by others. Many sexually abused patients, for example, have deep seated fears of being held unable to control their bodies and their fate.

These fears are broader than fear of dependency inasmuch as they relate to anticipation of complete loss of self and death. Clinicians may reassure patients that they will not become another person, lose their ability to control themselves, or even lose their ability to elect to stop taking medication. Highly creative people may fear (arguably correctly) that medication may dull their creative abilities, which are deeply tied with the person's sense of identity. Psychotherapy again may be necessary to address deeper cognitive blockages to accepting help because of fears of losing identity. In many cases, patients will need to consider and accept or reject trade-offs that come with taking medication.

5. *Side effects and fear of permanent injury:* Many patients do not understand that the risk of permanent side effects is relatively small with most medication. Clinicians can reassure patients that if there are unwanted side effects, stopping treatment will reverse most unwanted symptoms. Of course, some antipsychotic agents may cause permanent symptoms of tardive dyskinisia as well as potentially fatal loss of white blood cell production (agranulo cytosis, for example, or neuroleptic malignant syndrome). As relatively rare as these problems are, they should be discussed with patients for legal as well as ethical reasons while emphasizing that most unwanted effects are reversible.

Other medications, of course, can cause problems that lead to long-term consequences. Tricyclic antidepressants can produce orthostatic hypotension and consequent problems, especially for the elderly if they fall and break bones by standing up too quickly and fainting. But the negative effects of the medication itself can be reversed by quitting the medication, albeit gradually. The prescriber should not minimize these risks but can provide objective information about the risks of various medications.

Though the general negative side effects of medication can be explained in pamphlets and other handouts, the role of the prescribing clinician should be to understand the specific needs of individual patients. For example, the risk of falling is greater to the elderly and patients strongly concerned about body image will be more concerned than others about possible weight gain. Some patients will be especially distressed about loss of libido or orgasmic problems associated with SSRIGC's (serotonin reuptake inhibitors). Some patients may be especially bothered with problems associated with anticholinergic effects of many medications (constipation, dry mouth, urinary retention, and so forth), but others will tolerate these medications well or will be willing to do what is necessary (drink fluids, increase bulk intake) to overcome the unwanted effects.

Many patients who do not tolerate medication well may have low frustration tolerance or intolerance for discomfort. Cognitive therapy (*see* Burns, 1990) aimed at helping them counteract automatic "can't stand it" thoughts may be helpful for improvement of medication compliance. Other automatic thoughts can also interfere with compliance, such as "this should be easy," or "I shouldn't have to do what I do not want to do." The clinician should be able to tailor a message regarding these issues for each individual patient.

6. *Psychological reactance:* Many patients, especially those with dual diagnoses, may be psychologically reactant to authority and to the perception that their control and freedom are being limited (Harris and Watkins, 1986; Harris, 1995). Such patients are oppositional and passive-aggressive or passive-resistive and consequently refuse overtly or covertly to take medication as prescribed simply in reaction to the perception of coercion. Clinicians should be sensitive to appearing authoritarian and should develop cooperation and collaboration with the patient to avoid creating iatrogenic resistance to the prescription.

Patients who have antisocial features may be oppositional but also may have significant inability to bond or to trust because of early childhood experiences. Quite naturally, they are suspicious of doctors and doctors' recommendations. Of course, these patients are also most likely to seek medication that can be sold or abused, so special precautions are needed. It may be helpful to ask patients bluntly if they trust the clinician enough to follow advice. Getting the mistrust into the open may help the clinician find a way to explain the value of medication and encourage compliance.

7. *Stigma of mental illness:* Many patients resist medications that are for "psychiatric" problems because of the stigma associated with mental illness. It may be

helpful to refer to medication as "neurologic" rather than "psychiatric" and to help patients understand the interplay of social, psychological, and biological factors in all illnesses. For example, many important physical illnesses are, in fact, behaviorally based, such as lung cancer and heart disease, which are largely caused by unhealthy lifestyle choices. Many psychiatric illnesses are clearly "brain based" and are no different than any other disease of an organ, such as diabetes. Even illnesses that seem to be primarily a result of psychosocial stressors have affected the body and its organs physically, and this explanation may help patients understand the role of medication in their lives.

Patients often feel especially troubled and stigmatized at the prospect of taking medication for the remainder of their lives, whether it is for diabetes or a psychotic disorder. Many people can see the parallel between taking medication for psychiatric illnesses and life-long use of insulin for diabetes, a disease with which most people are somewhat familiar. Clinicians can help patients by drawing these analogies to other disease processes.

The expense and inconvenience of a permanent medication regimen are obvious reasons for patients' resistance. But additionally, the idea of having a permanent medication is interpreted by many people as an indication of their having an intrinsic defect. Many people who struggle with self-esteem and self-worth issues believe that they are intrinsically and inherently defective, and having to take medication life-long seems to symbolize their concerns and their fears about themselves. It may be helpful for these individuals to separate their illness from themselves by "externalizing" the illness. In this cognitive technique, patients develop a name for their illness to make it external from themselves and to allow them to refer to it as something apart from themselves. For example, a depressed person might refer to his or her depression as "The Doomsayer."

Certainly, the tendency of people to see themselves as defective is connected to depression itself but is also a factor in resistance to medication. Especially in depression, but in many other illnesses as well, patients personalize their problems and blame themselves, thus discounting the very real factors of depression that are outside their control, such as their biological makeup. The clinician can help patients by pointing out these unproductive ways of thinking, helping patients to develop methods to dispute the erroneous beliefs and thoughts and helping them to see the problem as external to their true selves.

8. *Other cognitive errors:* Other cognitive distortions may be strongly related to non-compliance with medication. For example, depressed patients predict the future pessimistically and dismiss the possibility that medication can help them. Or by using a mental filter, they exclude positive evidence that medication can work.

Even as patients take medication and begin to show behavioral improvement, they may discount the positive and focus only on remaining unchanged symptoms. If this tendency to discount positives is pointed out to patients prior to commencement of medication, the clinician can then remind the patient when such occurs. This is true of other cognitive errors as well, as outlined by Burns (1990).

9. *Perception that medication is unnecessary:* Many patients do not accept that they have an illness or that symptoms are serious enough to warrant medication (bipolar patients in manic states, for example). This resistance manifests itself when patients say they can work through their problems by themselves given enough time. Such resistance may reveal an underlying shame about accepting help.

Many patients, especially men, are taught that they should be self-reliant, and consequently medication is seen as a crutch that should be done without. Exploration with the patient of the collaborative role of the clinician may help to dispel some of these concerns, but deeper exploration of beliefs about when to accept help also may be necessary in some cases. It sometimes can be useful to find examples when the patient has used professional (in other words, legal) help and to explore why these are acceptable where psychiatric help is not.

10. *Fear from past experiences:* Many patients have had serious past medical and psychiatric illnesses that have required medication. The patient may have had severe reactions, producing a fear about taking any kind of medication. Many people have unpleasant memories of being forced to take medicine for common child illnesses and attach these memories to later contacts with doctors and other medical personnel. So it is not unexpected that many people have negative associations to medication. The clinician's role is to detoxify these early memories, in some cases by exploring these past experiences and

distinguishing them from the present situation. In other cases, reassurance may be all that is necessary, of course, but it is important to be alert to past medical history that may have created a "distaste" for medicine, including nonpsychiatric illnesses.

Many patients also have received misleading or outright false information about psychiatric treatment and medication from the media, including movies, magazines, and newspapers (Preston et al, 1994). It is difficult to overcome the fear that is generated when there is a report of someone becoming homicidal while on Prozac or Halcion, but it may be helpful to ask patients who seem reluctant if they have heard anything about their medication through the media. Sometimes, just bringing these reports out into the open helps defuse the patient's fear and anxiety. With more sophisticated patients, providing articles or summaries of research may be helpful to calm anxieties about the medication. Finally, though drug information provided by the manufacturer is necessarily comprehensive, many patients do not understand the legal reasons why manufacturers list every possible effect of the medication. It may be helpful to put this into perspective for the patient who is worried after reading such information.

11. *Cognitively unable to conform:* Some patients are simply unable to understand the instructions for their prescriptions. Others may be able to repeat the instructions but do not have sufficient mental capacity to anticipate the possible consequences of taking medicine inappropriately. Most people lack sufficient education and understanding of pharmacodynamic and pharmacokinetic principles to appreciate the significance of instructions for medication. A common example is that people take antibiotics only until they feel better, not realizing that it is important to complete the prescription to prevent bacterial infection from rebounding.

Psychiatric medication is no less complicated than medication prescribed by general practitioners, internists, and others. Stimmel (1997) outlined a number of general principles that should be discussed with patients, including:

a. when to expect an effect from medication
b. potential drug interactions
c. rare but serious adverse effects and what to do if encountered
d. what to do if a dose is missed
e. how long the drug will be needed

f. dietary restraints and how and whether to take the medication with food
g. what the medicine is for, expressed in terms the patient uses to describe his or her own illness and symptoms
h. when to expect beneficial side effects and adverse effects
i. why blood tests may be necessary
j. issues of dependence and withdrawal
k. PRN (as needed) use versus continuous dosing (for example, Buspar as an antianxiety medication cannot be taken as needed as can Xanax. However, not even Xanax is useful on an as-needed basis for panic attacks, because the panic typically has already subsided when the medication begins to work.)

Other topics that might be discussed include:

a. explanation of why doses should be taken at directed times of the day (in other words, some medications may produce soporific effects and therefore are better taken at night)
b. generic versus brand names
c. use of alcohol or other controlled but unprescribed substances while also taking medication
d. potential hazards of interaction with over-the-counter medications (which patients frequently think of as harmless)

12. *Wish to defeat the therapist:* In psychotherapy, many patients have an underlying transference of anger to treaters. These patients may have longstanding conflict with parents or other authority figures in their lives whom they wish to defeat. The anger manifests in a wish to defeat the treater by defying suggestions and refusing to get well. So with medication, patients gain victory from defeating the best efforts of their doctors. There is no easy solution to this problem, but it is possible that some suicides and overdoses result from patients seeking ultimate victory by killing themselves. Careful attention to past treatment failures may help the clinician develop strategies to prevent the patient from succeeding by overdosing. Such strategies might include allowing only nonlethal amounts of medication to be dispensed or giving injectable forms of medication. It is also likely that the therapist should remain concerned but not overinvested in treatment success; in this context, the patient achieves little by defeating the therapist.

13. *Lifestyle interference:* Taking medication and getting well sometimes prevents patients from doing other things they like, such as drinking alcohol. But medication also can interfere with other simple pleasures, such as sun bathing, and clinicians should attempt to anticipate how medication might interfere with the patient's daily routine and lifestyle.

In addition to lifestyle interference, the clinician should also note that changes in symptoms may deprive the patient of primary identification and gratification. The depressed patient, for example, may derive a great deal of secondary gain from being ill and may resist medication that produces gain that would ordinarily be seen by most people as positive. These issues are, of course, a central consideration in psychotherapy but are no less relevant to achieving success in treatment via medication.

Solutions to Noncompliance

Most doctors already do many of the things necessary to help patients take medication properly, but some review of these basics may be helpful.

1. *Patient education:* Patients need to be educated about the nature of their illness and the purpose of the medication. Psychiatric illnesses can often be compared to other, more easily recognized physical illnesses that require medication. Metaphors may help patients think about their neurological system as a computer or communications center in which neurotransmitters (medication) improve transmission.

It is also helpful to describe the purpose of the medication in terms of symptoms that the patient complains about. For example, if a person with schizophrenia is bothered by the voices he or she hears, then it may be good to discuss how the medication will help with this problem (Stimmel, 1997.) But if the patient is not bothered by the voices, then it will not motivate the client to promise relief from these auditory hallucinations.

2. *Cognitive restructuring:* Many patients have serious cognitive distortions that affect their use of medications. As previously mentioned, for example, some

patients discount positives and fail to see improvements that result from medication. Helping clients examine their thinking is an effective strategy.

Deeper cognitive restructuring needs to occur when patients' deep core beliefs in their worthlessness, defectiveness, and lack of trust in others create resistance to taking medication to get well. Clinicians need to be alert to the patient's psychological structure and anticipate how this structure may affect medication compliance. When prescribing physicians and psychotherapists work collaboratively, better communication about the patient can lead to better clinical understanding and monitoring of medication compliance and outcomes.

3. *Monitoring, support, and encouragement:* Most prescribers are so accustomed to psychiatric illnesses and medications that they lose sight of how unfamiliar patients are with these problems and remedies. Consequently, they may neglect what has always been a mainstay of medical and psychological treatment: the power of the human relationship. Hope and expectation in many cases are as powerful a potion as any drug in the medicine cabinet.

It is also important to recognize that patients have a great deal to do with the outcome of their treatment. Encouraging them to learn about and take charge of their illnesses can lead to better compliance with treatment recommendations as patients decide for themselves that they should adhere to a treatment regimen. Active participants learn far better than passive participants and will facilitate rather than impede treatment.

4. *Help with cost and inconvenience:* An effective treatment team comprises a doctor and social work staff intent on working with the whole person, including family and other social resources. Especially in these days of managed care, many psychiatric patients are too disorganized to manage the intricacies of insurance and the fragmented social service system. The most powerful drug becomes impotent if it cannot be properly taken because of funding problems or other blockages to compliance with recommended dosage and scheduling.

Summary

Psychoactive medication is an important part of psychiatric treatment, but medication is not something "done to" the patient. Rather, patients must be cooperatively and collaboratively involved in treatment. Clinicians will receive better feedback about the effects of prescriptions and will elicit less resistance to recommendations if patients are encouraged to be involved in treatment.

There are many practical reasons why patients do not take medication, such as cost and inconvenience. But there are also deeper psychological structures that create resistance and noncompliance, such as fear of dependency and loss of identify. Clinicians who do not try to understand their patients' personalities will have less effective treatment outcomes than clinicians who try to understand the person as an active agent whose choices and behavior will determine whether or not medication will be taken as prescribed.

REFERENCES

Burns, D. 1990. *The Feeling Good Handbook*. New York: Penguin Group.

Harris, G. and D. Watkins, 1986. *Counseling the Involuntary and Resistant Client*. Lanham, Maryland. American Correctional Association.

_____. 1995. *Overcoming Resistance: Success in Counseling Men*. Lanham, Maryland. American Correctional Association.

Preston, J., J. Heal, and M. Talaga. 1994. *Handbook of Clinical Psychopharmacology for Therapists*. Oakland, California: New Harbinger Publications, Inc.

Stimmel, G. 1997. What Patients Need to Know about Their Psychotropic Medication. Presentation to the International College of Prescribing Psychologists, *Prescribing Psychologists Register*, Las Vegas.

CHAPTER 10

Taking Care of Yourself in the Process:

Beverly Welo

Corrections Programs Therapist

Lino Lakes Correctional Facility

Lino Lakes, Minnesota

Counselor Self-care in Brutal Environments

"This is how people behave when their dailiness is destroyed, when for a few moments they see, plain and unadorned, one of the great shaping forces of life. Calamity fixes them with her mesmeric eyes and they begin to scoop and paw at the rubble of their days, trying to pluck the memory of the quotidian . . . from the garbage heaps of the irretrievable."

- Salman Rushdie, *The Ground Beneath Her Feet*

Helpers' neglect of their own needs for hopefulness, job satisfaction, and meaning in their work, contributes to their sense of despair, adds to the loss of clinicians who are gifted in their ability to work with difficult populations, and promotes staff burnout. The environments where staff encounter mandated clients are brutal by their nature, despite the best efforts of individual clinicians to mitigate the environment's effects on the therapeutic relationship. Working in brutal environments impacts clinicians physically, emotionally, and spiritually, making self-care an imperative. This chapter offers one clinician's story of self-neglect, self-care, and the renewal of hope within the confines of a brutal environment.

Encouraging introspection in resistant, mandated, or confined clients powerfully affects clinicians. Simply put, there is no way for you to provide the opportunity for others to find their pain without your own pain finding you. This chapter will not attempt to explore all of the aspects of vicarious traumatization to which therapists are prey. The best sourcebook for a complete discussion of this issue is *Trauma and the Therapist* (Pearlman and Saakvitne, 1995). My goal is simply to speak directly to practitioners who work in corrections, most particularly those who provide grief and loss counseling to incarcerated men. I am offering my journey in the hope that others may profit from it.

Never Forget Your Own Ability to Suffer

In *Healing Pain: Attachment, Loss and Grief Therapy* (1991), Marianne-Davidson Nielson and Nini Leick counsel grief therapists thus: "If we are to convince our clients that the necessary pain contains a healthy process, we have to believe this ourselves." However, our belief in the process is not seen to be sufficient. They emphasize, "A natural consequence of this is that the therapist must have worked through his own grief in order to help others work with theirs." This is sound advice, certainly; yet, the notion of having worked through all of our griefs seems superhuman.

Unexpected haunting by a long buried grief is something I have experienced many times while doing this work. Recently, a man sat in front of me struggling to come to grips with the loss of his dreams of being a professional athlete. His pain was clearly genuine as he passionately described the coaches who had urged him to play while injured, the sexual carnival his athletic ability had given him access to, the hopes his family had placed on him, and the physical gifts his body had seemed to possess in unlimited quantity. He painfully acknowledged the final, irreparable injury followed by the wholesale desertion of his fans, lovers, coaches, and family; meanwhile, across the desk, I had begun reliving a loss a distant childhood away.

My loss was not even remotely connected to the events that he was revealing, but a memory had been triggered by his statement, "He looked at me like I was a stranger." I was remembering a little girl on a playground whose friend was suddenly no longer her friend. Once remembered, the memory filled me with an intense sadness. Pain is pain, and no matter how distant from you an experience described by a client appears to be, distance will not guarantee your comfort.

The question, then, was what to do with this new information? My first impulse was to shunt the memories aside, in order to proceed with the interview without my humanity (or vulnerability) leaking through. My second thought was experienced in the urge to reveal this information to the client, to join him by shared experience. I have learned to challenge these initial impulses and filter them through my understanding of an appropriate corrections relationship. I selected a different method of joining—acknowledgement of the fact that I did not share his history. I said something to this effect, "I have not had your experiences, I don't presume to say I understand, but pain is pain. I have experienced the confusion of relationships suddenly ending, successes drifting away, and injuries that left me thinking my body had betrayed me. What we need to do is search through the rubble of these events to see if anything of value can be found."

The initial impulses (discarding the memories or allowing myself to process a loss of my own with a client) are both "traps" in which therapists new to corrections can find themselves. Each corrections clinician needs the direction of seasoned guides in order to serve their clients appropriately and build a mutually satisfying therapeutic relationship. My guides have served me well. I hope that readers will allow my experiences to provide signposts on their journeys.

Bringing Your Pain through the Sallyport

The sallyport is the name given to the progression of clanging metal doors that give egress to most American prisons. In the medium-custody facility at Lino Lakes, Minnesota, the sallyport is where my ID badge is swiped and my hand is examined by a machine to determine that I am, in fact, a staff member. Before I enter the prison each morning, the contents of my bag, and the menu of my lunch, are duly noted by a corrections officer. At times, it has seemed to me that stepping through that portal separated me from my own inner life as well. I don a carefully construct-ed professional manner, I endeavor to be "firm and fair" with my inmate clients, and the workload is such that I frequently go through the day without "personal" interac-tions of any kind. Some days it is only when the staff are queuing up for our return through the sallyport that we have a minute to ask after each other's children, com-miserate with a coworker who is juggling an impossible workload, or notice that the get-well card we are all signing is for someone we have sworn to lunch with for the past six months. I am grateful for the twenty-minute commute ahead of me, it gives me a chance to come back to my "dailiness," my sense of self outside of the prison environment.

But the walk through the sallyport does not always find me sufficiently "buttoned up" to be safe from the brutality of the prison's environment. The untimely death of my mother, the painful end of a cherished relationship, illness, and stress have all led me to feel, at times, that my therapeutic stance was insufficient for the task of self-protection. It is at moments like this that my professional demeanor threatens to become a rigid mask, rather than a flexible attitude that is valuable to my clients as well as myself.

While doing your work, you will naturally also have to experience present losses that tax your strength even more than the "old" pain. You may find (as I have) that just as you are congratulating yourself on having the strength to return to a difficult and unforgiving environment, you will repeatedly be sent clients whose experience of a death, relationship loss, or family crisis will precisely replicate your own grief. As they ask, "Why, why, why?" all of your answers will seem clichéd, even preposter-ous to you. Yet, they are the only answers that you have. It is at these moments that the urge to process my own losses with clients has been most profound. If that boundary were to be crossed, the results would most certainly damage the therapeu-tic relationship, and might actively harm my client or myself.

In *Questions and Answers on Death and Dying*, Kubler-Ross bravely asserted, "I dare to get emotionally involved . . . this saves me the trouble of using half of my energy to cover up my feelings." But her clients were not the raging grievers you encounter daily.

Can you afford to weep with your clients? Share with them stories of your own pain, confusion and suffering? Allow yourself that kind of vulnerability with men who are violent, predatory, and masters of manipulation? You will have to make your own decision in these matters, but I have answered the questions above with a qualified "Yes."

Believing in the Process, While Keeping Your Soul Whole

A lifelong friend recently gave me a generous compliment. She said that I shared, in common with her, "the courage to be vulnerable." She spoke of courage, not fool-hardiness. Caregivers who believe that they cannot be harmed by the immense tide of human suffering that difficult work environments force upon them are not only foolhardy, they are showing dangerous signs of hubris—the overweening pride that led to catastrophic results for Oedipus and his family. The humility with which I approach my work has a practical consideration at its base; I have seen the effects, on myself as well as others, which a hubristic belief in complete self-protection has had.

Therefore, I choose my moments of vulnerability with great care. If I choose, for example, to reveal some aspect of my own journey to illuminate a concept in the classroom, I do so only when I am certain that I will be able to adequately distance myself from the power of the loss. During the intensity of group therapy, my self-disclosure is often disguised to safely distance it from me. In the intimacy of a one-on-one session, I remain willing to shed tears when compassion prompts them, but I choose not to disclose any particulars of my own losses in that setting.

At times, I have used my own experiences, but distanced myself from them by disguising them as "stories." In the workbook, *Life Beyond Loss* (Welo, 1999), clients are encouraged to write stories about ways that they "might" deal with loss different-ly. This technique allows them to examine the potential benefits of introspection without being overwhelmed by a long buried grief. In the same way that your clients can be brought into experiencing the pain of a loss by telling a story and revealing their lost pain to themselves in the process, you can establish distance by using the technique in reverse. I have protected my anonymity, or that of friends and family members, by changing their sex, race, or age so dramatically that they would be unrecognizable even to themselves.

In describing self-disclosure, I do not want to intimate that it is ever appropriate to work through a grief of your own with a client. Ethically, this is completely unsupportable. Besides, you might end up being taken care of by the inmates, who traditionally are not practitioners likely to serve you well. Even the most ethical therapist can be drawn into this unlikely behavior without supervision and case consultation. If your agency does not adequately provide such services, it is imperative to develop working relationships with peers who are sufficiently intimate to encourage frank discussion of countertransference issues. The surest way to "take your own pulse" in these matters is to review your caseload for clients who engender strong emotional responses in you; those whose progress, or lack of progress, you see as a direct reflection of your skills.

Developing Collegial Relationships

Developing relationships with colleagues that are intimate enough to allow frank discussion of countertransference issues is a difficult process in any workplace. The corrections model, based as it is on a hierarchical military system, is an especially difficult environment for soliciting this type of feedback. I have been inordinately blessed with supervisors who have facilitated self-examination and fostered an environment where challenge of staff choices in treatment planning can be framed in the context of countertransference, but this is clearly not always the case.

Individual therapists who are new to corrections will likely find the barracks humor and playful (or not so playful) jabs from coworkers disconcerting. It takes a while for new clinicians to be seen by correctional peers as up to the task at hand. Turnover of new staff is common, and uncertainty regarding a new clinician's commitment to corrections may keep coworkers at a distance. An old corrections adage regarding the rookie's point of view towards inmates is, "The first year they can't do enough for them, the second year that can't do enough to them," pretty well sums up the dangers of allowing inmate clients too free a rein, followed by punishing them for taking you for a ride.

"We didn't break 'em and we can't fix 'em," is another corrections adage that has often helped me to see my clients more clearly. I imagine the succession of helpers who came before me: parents or foster parents, teachers, coaches, therapists, clergy, and others. It is extremely rare to encounter a corrections client who has never been encouraged, confronted, or aided before I came onto the scene. Our clients make choices, among them the choice to accept or reject the help that is offered. Therapists need to be able to humbly acknowledge their limitations, or risk having a mistaken belief in their own abilities actually harm their clients. This is true in any clinical setting, but corrections professionals must always remain cognizant of the fact that our clients have actively sought to harm others. This level of client dangerousness gives our work a heightened stress as we seek to minimize the likelihood of it reoccurring. We are not responsible for our client's choices, but we are responsible for our own choices, including our acknowledgment of our limitations.

Soul Injuries through Overdisclosure and The Effects of a Brutal Environment

Naturally enough, I could not have developed the structure outlined above without having first crossed my own boundaries and learning the pain of overdisclosure. Several years ago, I was introducing the grief issues discussed in *Life Beyond Loss* to a large group of men in the prison education building. The twenty-five or thirty men in attendance were there for a ninety-minute lecture, and they were all strangers to me. I wanted to create a kind of "instant" therapeutic bond, and I used self-disclosure to accomplish my goal. I talked about my mother's death and then found myself extremely uncomfortable with the level of sadness and vulnerability I felt as I spoke.

In retrospect, it is clear that in my rush to establish credibility with the men, I had forgotten that a therapeutic alliance requires both parties' participation. Self-disclosure should never be self-sacrifice, that is the way of the therapist-martyr, and a sure path to burnout. Scolding myself for being a bad therapist did not seem an effective way to deal with my overdisclosure. I sought guidance from my own therapist, learned a painful lesson, and ultimately forgave myself for being human. Over the intervening years, I overdisclosed less and less often, but each time the injuries were as real as any other wounds, requiring healing, self-forgiveness, therapeutic intervention, and time.

Brutality

Prisons are brutal environments. It seems that this should go without saying, yet a "normalization" process goes on for us all as we work in the field of corrections. When I think back to my first year in the prison, I know I was shocked to find myself behind the razor wire; yet, I took a perverse pride in it as well—as if it proved I was one tough cookie.

Very quickly, the shock wore off; I no longer saw the sallyport, the razor wire, the drug-sniffing dogs, the shackles, or the holding cells—it was all just "work." Lino Lakes is a medium-security prison and much of it, is visible from a nearby highway. There's no brick wall surrounding it—just the gleaming razor wire. In time I lulled myself into the illusion that being in the prison did not bother me at all. But it did bother me, it bothered my dreams and my wakefulness and it gave me a skewed view of brutality. I am proud to be working at Lino Lakes. The environment is as humane, respectful, and secure as any prison in the United States. But prison is prison, and the loss of freedom is, in itself, a brutal reality.

There is the brutality of all that I hear, or read, as part of my work with the inmates. The horror stories of their crimes, the victim impact statements, the anguish of their family members, and the dry legalese that ascribes a number of days computed to match a degree of criminality. All of these elements contribute to the stress and pain of working behind the razor wire. Clients who recidivate are also a source of pain, whether they return to prison because the have reoffended, or "only" because they have violated the conditions of their release. It is painful to see them return simply because they have once again injured all of those who care for them.

As I work with the inmates on their loss histories, I see the brutality of their child-hoods; the abuse, neglect, sexual assault, shame, addiction, and hopelessness they were raised with is often literally horrifying. Their suffering cannot ever excuse their perpetration, but it is suffering just the same. At times, I hear or read something that strikes at the core of my being with such force that I fear my soul itself is damaged. I believe it is the grief work I do that saves me from soul destruction, just as it threatens to overwhelm me with the horrors it unearths. The grief work allows me to see the genuine pain in the men I work with and to view them as fellow sufferers—just as the workbook encourages them to do this with others.

Like many of life's mysteries, the question and the answer lie together in the same place—it is because the environment is so brutal that compassion can flourish, and it is because compassionate helpers are there that we can be so badly wounded. Do not undervalue the toll that the brutality of your environment may be taking on you.

How to Work in a Brutal Environment without Becoming a Brute

Cultivate loving friendships among your coworkers. Decorate your office or cubicle with photographs that show love, hope, tenderness, and joy. Cry on coworkers' shoulders and encourage them to cry on yours. Pray. See your own therapist. Force yourself to take a walk after work, no matter how tired you are. Remember that your body is the only thing you'll ever own, value it. Love your children. Notice when success happens.

How to Make a Brutal Environment Worse

Compete with your coworkers to see who can do the most work with the least enjoyment. Decorate your office or cubicle with memos and to-do lists. When you are wounded, shame yourself. When a coworker appears wounded, think of her or him as being "unprofessional." Blame God. Need no one. Go home, sit on the couch and watch TV. Smoke, drink, and eat to excess. Believe your family doesn't appreciate you enough. Be the most cynical person you have ever known—and think of it as a benefit.

Because I was already a recovering alcoholic when I began my work in corrections, I have never drunk alcohol to numb the pain. Other than not drinking, I have done at least some of everything listed in the two paragraphs above. They both work.

Know Your Limits

If a present grief is very painful, you might request to take a hiatus from some aspects of your work, or share your duties with a peer. I was able to take several weeks off from a grief and loss psychoeducational class after the death of my mother—but I know that resources are stretched to the limit everywhere, and this may not always be possible. Her death was such a powerful loss for me that those weeks flew by in a second. The overdisclosure I mentioned above occurred nearly two years after her death. I had misjudged the vulnerability that discussion of that loss (in that environment) would bring up in me.

Following a painful separation, I actually left corrections for six months. By that time, I had been in the corrections field for a number of years and I was able to evaluate my vulnerability more clearly. I knew that I was too vulnerable to be safe in a corrections environment; I also knew that my vulnerability would put other staff at risk. When I returned, I savored the deep sense of kinship I had for my fellow corrections workers. I regained the sense of purpose I had lost in my grief, and I was able to function safely in the corrections environment again.

On those occasions when you know yourself to be significantly vulnerable, and a leave or re-assignment is not possible, I suggest an absolute ban on self-disclosure with clients. I also suggest that you make use of your EAP and any other support systems that are available to you. Brief or long-term therapy may provide the support you need to continue in your day-to-day duties. Therapists are often as resistant to the notion of needing therapeutic interventions as their clients. Recognizing the need for help is doubly difficult in correctional environments, with their emphasis on self-reliance. Please give yourself permission to seek therapeutic aid when needed. For those whose workplace does not offer case consultation, the benefits of a therapeutic journey can be even more significant. A personal therapist can offer you the opportunity to consult regarding countertransference issues and vicarious traumatization, as well as remind you of the importance of balance, self-forgiveness, and self-regard.

Finally, and most drastically, know you can leave your job if it is the only healthy alternative for you. I doubt that my suggestion will cause numbers of you to take this course of action—I could not make the suggestion in good conscience if I did. But all helpers need to have the humility to realize that we are replaceable. If your job threatens your soul, do not hesitate to acknowledge it. Burnout is very real; we've all seen it. Whistling by the graveyard, or promising ourselves it will not happen to us is how all the burned-out helpers we have ever worked with keep coming to their desks every day. We deserve all the support we can get, and we owe it to ourselves, our families, and our clients to ask for help when we need it.

In closing, I would like to say that I have written this chapter in the hope that it will be of assistance to those entering the field of corrections. My personal belief is that our work has great value to our society, whether its focus is chemical dependency treatment, sex offender treatment, psychological services, or pastoral care. This brief overview of my experiences is offered with the desire to aid and comfort. As the numbers of incarcerated men and women in this country rise to dizzying heights, very few stop to consider the men and women who provide services for the incarcerated. I think about us all the time, wish us well, and hope we all make it safely through another day.

REFERENCES

Kubler-Ross, E. 1975. *Questions and Answers on Death and Dying.* Englewood Cliffs, New Jersey: Prentice-Hall.

Leick, N. and M. Davidson-Nielson. 1991 *Healing Pain: Attachment, Loss and Grief Therapy.* London: Tavistock.

Pearlman, A. P. and L. A. Saakvitne. 1995. *Trauma and the Therapist: Countertransference and Vicarious Traumatization in Psychotherapy with Incest Survivors.* New York: Norton.

Welo, B. K. 1999. *Life Beyond Loss: A Workbook for Incarcerated Men, Revised Edition.* Lanham, Maryland: American Correctional Association.

_____. *Raging Grievers: A Caregivers Guide to Providing Grief and Loss Work for Incarcerated Men.* Unpublished manuscript.

About the Authors

ABOUT THE AUTHORS

Gary L. Donovan

Gary L. Donovan is the director of the Career Center, University of Minnesota, Morris. He also is the Clinical Supervisor for Counseling Associates of West Central Minnesota, an outpatient mental health office of the Swift County-Benson Hospital.

George A. Harris

George A. Harris is a licensed psychologist in private practice in Kansas City where he provides counseling and evaluation services. He has been a psychologist in vocational rehabilitation and correctional programs and was an associate professor at Washburn University in Topeka, Kansas. His first book, *Broken Ears, Wounded Hearts*, was selected as best book of 1984 by the President's Committee on Employment of the Handicapped. He coauthored *Marketing Professional Services through Advertising*, which was an alternate selection of the Behavioral Sciences Book Club. He has written and edited three books on counseling difficult clients, including his most recent, *Overcoming Resistance: Success in Counseling Men*. He wrote a screenplay for a video produced by Knowles Law Book Company on legal and psychological implications of divorce. He has written a variety of professional and trade publication articles on subjects ranging from domestic violence to managing stress.

Jerry Larke

Dr. Jerry Larke is a psychologist in private practice in Marshfield, Massachusetts.

Victor S. Lombardo

Dr. Victor S. Lombardo is a tenured professor and associate director of the International Center for the Study and Treatment of Delinquent and Criminal Behavior at the Marshall University Graduate College in South Charleston, West Virginia. He also is a member of the doctoral faculty at West Virginia University. His educational background includes training in cognitive and developmental psychology with a focus in education and treatment of the emotionally disturbed and socially maladjusted, the learning disabled, and other exceptional populations. He is a best-selling author with more than 200 international refereed publications. Nationally and internationally he trains in rational cognitive therapy (RCT), self-defense, deescalation, and hostage negotiation tactics, which he has been doing for more than thirty years.

Flynn O'Malley

Dr. Flynn O'Malley, a clinical psychologist, received his Ph.D. from the University of New Mexico in 1976. He is a Diplomate in Clinical Psychology of the American Board of Professional Psychology. Since 1981, Dr. O'Malley has been on the clinical staff of the Menninger Clinic in Topeka, Kansas. He currently serves as the director of Outpatient Services. Dr. O'Malley has presented at national, regional, and local meetings of professional organizations; conducted workshops and consulted for hospitals, agencies, schools, and other health and service facilities; lectured at universities and other educational institutions; and has appeared on national and regional media programs.

Floyd F. Robison

Floyd F. Robison is an associate professor in the Department of Counseling and Educational Psychology, Indiana University, Indianapolis, Indiana. His research includes gerontological counseling, therapeutic group counseling, and family counseling.

Marlow H. Smaby

Marlow H. Smaby is a professor and chairperson of the Department of Counseling and Educational Psychology, University of Nevada, Reno. His research addresses performance assessment methods in the preparation of professional counselors.

Robert Smith

Dr. Robert R. Smith is a tenured professor of counseling and leadership studies and director and cofounder of the International Center for the Study and Treatment of Delinquent Criminal Behavior at Marshall University Graduate College in South Charleston, West Virginia. He is also a member of the doctoral faculty at West Virginia University. Dr. Smith's education background includes training in cognitive and developmental psychology with focuses on delinquents, criminals, and other at-risk populations. He is a best-selling author of more than 100 international refereed publications. He trains staff in correctional, mental health, school, volunteer programs, and other settings. He is also a licensed professional counselor and a national board certified counselor.

Pam Stanchfield

Pam Stanchfield is a senior therapist in the Sex Offender Treatment Program (SOTP) at the medium-custody correctional facility at Lino Lakes, Minnesota. At SOTP, she facilitates the aftercare component of the program, as well as an intensive treatment track. She is currently at work on *Zen and the Art of Sex Offender Therapy*.

Glenn D. Walters

Glenn D. Walters received his Ph.D. in counseling psychology from Texas Tech University in 1982 after completing a one-year predoctoral internship in clinical psychology at the Dwight David Eisenhower Army Medical Center in Fort Gordon, Georgia. He has worked in the corrections field since 1983 and published approximately 100 articles and ten books, including *The Criminal Lifestyle* (Sage, 1990) and *Changing Lives of Crime and Drugs: Intervening with the Substance Abusing Criminal Offender* (Wiley, 1998). Dr. Walters' current research interests include genetic studies on crime, alcoholism, and problem gambling; further development of the Psychological Inventory of Criminal Thinking Styles; and the creation of a general theory of lifestyles.

Beverly Welo

Beverly Welo is a corrections program therapist in the Treatment, Recovery and Independence from Alcohol and Drugs (TRIAD) chemical dependency program located in the medium-custody correctional facility at Lino Lakes, Minnesota. In addition to these duties, she lectures on grief and loss issues and conducts grief groups for inmates. She is the author of *Life Beyond Loss: A Workbook for Incarcerated Men*. She is currently at work on *Raging Grievers: A Caregiver's Guide to Providing Grief and Loss Work for Incarcerated Men*.

INDEX

A

B

C

Avoid the Offender's Well Placed Traps

The Art of the Con: Avoiding Offender Manipulation

Gary F. Cornelius

Many officers and staff believe they are too smart to be tricked by an offender. Realizing this possibility is the first step in avoiding manipulation. This book has two goals. First, to provide the corrections professional with a better understanding of offenders and their characteristics, behavior and culture. Second, Cornelius shows how staff and volunteers can maintain power, authority and control by resisting manipulation. Divided into six chapters, each contains the central theme of manipulation — how the criminal offender will attempt to circumvent supervision by correctional staff – and includes true examples. The concepts in this book apply to everyone in the field, and show how manipulation can occur in prisons, jails or community supervision. Appendices are included to help with training. (2001, 128 pages, 1-56991-147-9)

#759-TC1 • Nonmembers $18.00 • ACA members $14.40

"This would be an excellent training book for new employees in a state prison, county jail or probation department."

John D. Morgan
Warden, North Central Correctional Institution
Marion, Ohio

Call 1-800-222-5646, ext. 1860 to order!
American Correctional Association
4380 Forbes Boulevard
Lanham, MD 20706-4322

FOUNDED 1870

Counseling Resources
for Treating Today's Offenders

Correctional Assessment, Casework
& Counseling, 3rd Edition
Anthony Walsh, Ph.D.

This updated edition covers practical interviewing and counseling skills, including how to adapt counseling theories to
community or institutional corrections, and how to supervise
the alcoholic, drug addict, sex offender, schizophrenic, and
mentally immature client. Sample case materials, such as
pre-sentence reports, sentencing guidelines, classification
scales, and risk and needs scales give readers an understanding of the actual
assessment process. This edition includes an expanded section on the legal
issues involved in counseling these individuals. Walsh has incorporated the lat-
est research and data to ensure this manual remains timely. An instructor's
manual is available with the purchase of 10 or more books. (2001, 543 pages,
index, 1-56991-133-9)
#450-TC1   • Nonmembers $34.95 • ACA members $27.95

Changing Criminal Thinking:
A Treatment Program
Boyd D. Sharp, MS, LPC

This book provides an account of a successful treatment
program for counselors to use in a correctional setting. The
program focuses on the pretense that criminals think differently than prosocial people. Most offenders in the United
States will eventually be released, but in many cases the
criminal mind is still intact. These offenders must be rehabil-
itated in order to conform with society. Sharp combines the
theory of why the program works with specific examples of his experiences. He
includes explanations on how others can develop and implement such a program. (2000, 168 pages, 1-56991-125-8)
#718-TC1   • Nonmembers $23.00 • ACA members $18.40

• •

FOUNDED 1870

1-800-222-5646, ext. 1860
American Correctional Association
4380 Forbes Boulevard
Lanham, MD 20706
www.aca.org